F-111

Fort Worth Swinger

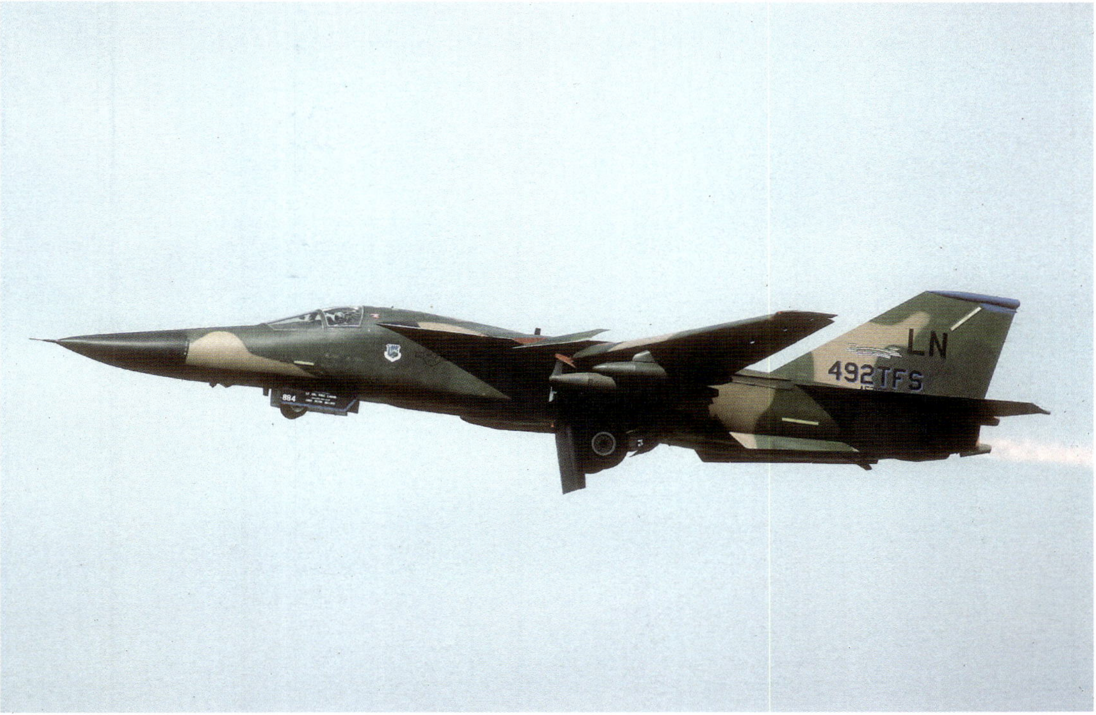

BOB ARCHER

KEY Books

HISTORIC MILITARY AIRCRAFT SERIES, VOLUME 3

Title page image: F-111F 71-0884 of the 492nd TFS commander departing Fairford in July 1991. The WSO aboard this aircraft is the late Capt (later Major) Troy Campbell, who was a friend and volunteer colleague at Royal International Air Tattoo (RIAT) for several years. (Bob Archer)

Contents page image: A pair of 42nd Electronic Combat Squadron EF-111As, serials 67-0048 and 66-0049, over Turkey during March 1991 while flying from Incirlik Air Base. (T Laurent)

Major Troy Campbell

Dedication

This book is dedicated to my friend, colleague, and fellow volunteer at the Royal International Air Tattoo, the late Major Troy Campbell (USAF retired). Troy was a Weapons Systems Officer with two tours at RAF Lakenheath, crewing F-111Fs, and later F-15Es. He participated in Operation *Desert Storm*, the first Gulf War, flying 30 combat sorties against Iraqi targets. Subsequently, he flew in Operation *Provide Comfort* over Iraq and Operation *Deny Flight* above Bosnia. During 9/11, Troy took his turn protecting the skies above Washington, D.C. flying the F-15E, while stationed at Seymour-Johnson AFB, North Carolina.

Acknowledgements

Much of the information presented here has been obtained from a host of publications. The primary source is, of course, *British Aviation Review* (BAR), which has become the 'military aviation researcher's bible'. BAR recorded, in great detail, events from the period when military aviation was at its pinnacle. Without the diligence of the BAR team, much information would not be so readily available. I am also indebted to the late Jim Freidhoff for conscientiously trawling the corridors of various military offices in Washington to eventually unearth the wondrous document containing full details of the USAF/USN aircraft losses in the Vietnam War. The information concerning F-111 accidents/losses presented here was obtained by Jim. Other sources of data have included books produced by both military historians, as well as enthusiasts, which are too numerous to list. However, three friends who deserve special praise for tail-code information are Philippe Lamberts in Belgium, Pat Martin in Canada and Brian Rogers in Kansas. Furthermore, the late Doug Remington studied this subject and was instrumental in compiling detailed listings upon which much of the written works are based. Others who deserve mention for their assistance are former F-111 aircrew Don Logan and Jim Rotromel, both of whom provided a wealth of detail.

A great many hours were spent by the author sitting outside air bases to record and photograph F-111s. While this may have seemed fruitless at the time, the data recorded has proved to be priceless. Finally, I wish to acknowledge my fellow enthusiasts and travelling companions in the UK who deserve recognition. These friends include Paul Bennett, Pete Foster, Paul Goddard, Steve Hill, Colin Johnson, Lindsay Peacock, Chris Pocock, Geoff Rhodes, Chris Russell and Dave Wilton. Paul Bennett, in particular, was influential in guiding me in the art of photography. Finally, I say a huge thank you to Steve Hill for his support with enhancing imagery.

While a lot of illustrations are from the author's own collection, this book would not have been possible without the help of many other photographers, with due credit against each image where known. To all of these photographers I extend my grateful thanks. In certain instances, the original photographer is unknown, so apologies are extended for this situation. Furthermore, I wish to say a heartfelt thank you to all the public affairs officers at numerous air bases worldwide, who kindly permitted access to their facilities over the last 50 years. Without their help, this book would have far fewer illustrations.

Published by Key Books
An imprint of Key Publishing Ltd
PO Box 100
Stamford
Lincs PE19 1XQ

www.keypublishing.com

The right of Bob Archer to be identified as the author of this book has been asserted in accordance with the Copyright, Designs and Patents Act 1988 Sections 77 and 78.

Copyright © Bob Archer, 2021

ISBN 978 1 913870 63 8

All rights reserved. Reproduction in whole or in part in any form whatsoever or by any means is strictly prohibited without the prior permission of the Publisher.

Typeset by SJmagic DESIGN SERVICES, India.

Contents

Introduction		4
Chapter 1	A Shaky Beginning	6
Chapter 2	The F-111A	12
Chapter 3	The F-111B and F-111D	18
Chapter 4	The F-111E	23
Chapter 5	The F-111F	32
Chapter 6	The F-111G and EF-111A	45
Chapter 7	The FB-111A	51
Chapter 8	The F-111 in Foreign Service	60
Chapter 9	Final Days	69
Chapter 10	Conclusion	75
Appendix		83

Introduction

The F-111 has been the subject of previous books, although most were written before the final aircraft had completed their service careers. The purpose of this book is to chronicle details of operations, colour schemes and markings to the very end. The F-111 was revolutionary at the time of its introduction into service and was, without doubt, an extremely popular aircraft, with both military personnel and the enthusiast community. Capable of delivering a wide variety of ordnance, and with a high degree of survivability, the F-111 not only looked right, it was right – arguably the best tactical aircraft for the deterrence mission at the time. Details of the technicalities involved and the lengthy development programme have been covered extensively in other books and are therefore not repeated here. The purpose of this publication is to pick up the story from the period when the test agenda evolved into aircraft joining operational squadrons through to the period of retirement. However, while technical features are mostly excluded, relevant background details, touching on this area, are incorporated where necessary.

F-111E 68-0002 of the 79th TFS wearing colourful nose art and named *Imperial Wizard*. (Paul Crickmore)

474th TFW F-111A 67-0105 overflying the Nevada wilderness in May 1976. Note the two red banners beneath the cockpit, one for the assigned pilot and the other for the dedicated crew chief. (Don Logan)

The design requirements were groundbreaking, but as the parameters were etched onto the drawing boards, the reality of the difficulties of incorporating these prerequisites began to become evident. The proposal was to meet the ideals of both the Navy and the Air Force within a single, basic fighter design. This prospect, in reality, was never going to work and was always going to be fraught with disagreement right from the start. Nevertheless, through steadfast dedication by the Air Force, the F-111 eventually entered service. Furthermore, steely determination on the part of the manufacturer, as well as the test establishments, ensured problems were overcome, and the F-111 proved to be a resounding success.

So why the title Fort Worth Swinger? Well, quite simply, the F-111 was produced at the giant General Dynamics (GD) plant in Fort Worth, Texas. And Swinger? The swing-wing F-111 had a variety of nicknames, one of which was 'Swinger', applied by enthusiasts in the UK. This was during the period when the type was commonplace with the United States Air Forces in Europe (USAFE). The authorities eventually applied the name Aardvark, but this was not until the latter period of service.

Ten Different F-111 Versions

For ease of reference, in this book details of operations, unit assignments and colour schemes are presented within each specific version. There were five operational USAF models in the tactical role (F-111A, F-111D, F-111E, F-111F and F-111G), one performing a strategic mission (FB-111A), an electronic warfare version (EF-111A) along with a single export order (F-111C), which is covered in chapter 8. Non-operational versions were the Navy's F-111B and the F-111K model for the UK. These are presented in suffix order, with the two specialist models after F-111G.

Chapter 1
A Shaky Beginning

The twentieth century was the decade that ushered the aeroplane into everyday life, initially fabricated from little more than wood and wire, but gradually evolving into an unparalleled transportation system. Many aircraft types transitioned from the drawing board to production relatively smoothly. Others endured a gestation period that was beset with problems and came within a whisker of being terminated. Two American designs that fall into the latter category are the Lockheed C-5 Galaxy and the General Dynamics F-111 Aardvark. Both suffered major cost overruns, due to the requirement for considerable rectifications before they were declared fit for entry into service. And, unsurprisingly, both became hugely successful at their respective tasks.

Whereas the C-5 continues in service, with a career that will likely span a further 20 years, the F-111 has been retired from service, but did not bow out before achieving a triumphant combat role during the first Gulf War. Earlier, the F-111 had been deployed to Vietnam but endured an ignominious debut, primarily operating in an environment for which it had been envisaged but flown by aircrew who were not experienced in combat. After a quick withdrawal, and an urgent review, the aircraft subsequently returned some years later and proved to be much more successful the second time around.

Air Force vs Navy Disagreements

The F-111 was the result of a series of operational requirements for a new fighter-bomber which could replace several existing late 1940s/early 1950s designs, incorporating current and perceived technology. In December 1960, the project gained the name Tactical Fighter Experimental (TFX). Soon afterwards, new Secretary of Defense Robert Strange McNamara asked the Army and Navy to combine with the Air Force for a joint capability. The Air Force requirement was for a fighter-bomber to perform interdiction of enemy logistics but that could also conduct close air support (CAS) of ground troops for the Army. The Navy's primary need was for an air defence fighter for the fleet. McNamara believed that, collectively, these capabilities performed by a single tri-service fighter offered the prospect to reap financial benefits. He was the prime supporter of this concept as an effective method of satisfying several tasks with a single design. The potential cost savings in development alone were expected to be significant. Additionally, the unit cost for a large production run would also be appreciably less than the individual services having a separate design.

Historically significant F-111 66-0016 was the fourth operational Aardvark to be delivered, joining the 474th TFW on 27 November 1967. One of the Combat Lancer deployment to Thailand in 1968, it flew the first combat mission on 18 March. Seen at Nellis AFB in October 1975. (Bob Archer)

Eventually, the Army's CAS stipulation was dropped, while, unsurprisingly, the Navy and Air Force were unable to agree a final requirement. Undeterred, McNamara remained convinced, ordering the two services to find common ground. Ultimately, a Request For Proposals was issued in September 1961 to the top ten aircraft manufacturers. Nine responded, with the Boeing proposition being chosen by the two services' representatives, although this was rejected by the Air Force Council. Despite no clear winner, it was agreed the Boeing and GDs' propositions warranted further examination. Funds were allocated to both companies for additional design details. Further disagreements culminated in McNamara ordering a run-off based on commonality of capability, cost and performance. Again, Boeing was declared the winner by the Air Force Council, but politics intervened, with McNamara siding with GD. There were suggestions that the all-powerful Texas congressional lobby, possibly colluding with Texan-born Vice President Lyndon Johnson, ruled in favour of GD, thereby securing jobs at its Fort Worth facility.

F-111 Designation Allocated

The TFX received official designations in December 1961, with the Air Force allocating its as the F-111A, while the Navy used the title F-111B. On 21 December 1962, the first contract was awarded, although with costs beginning to escalate, a radical rethink of certain aspects of the programme was necessary. Various lesser roles were abandoned as the project began to suffer from a surfeit of new technology trying to be incorporated within the limitations of budget, time constraints and airframe space.

In spite of these problems, the Air Force began procurement, forming the Research, Development, Test and Evaluation (RDT&E) programme office tasked with this aspect of pre-production assessment. At this time, production was expected to be 431 aircraft – fewer than half the number originally anticipated. The expectation was subsequently amended to a fixed price, incentive firm contract, covering 493 airframes. They consisted of 445 F-111s for the Air Force, including 50 being acquired for the Royal Air Force, 24 Navy F-111Bs (subsequently reduced to just two, when the service abandoned the programme) and 24 for Australia.

Shortcomings notwithstanding, the first F-111A 63-9766 was accepted by the Air Force on 21 December 1964 and was engaged in test duties, along with the next 29 airframes. 63-9766 had a very limited career, only flying 253 hours during just 210 flights. The final flight was on 5 August 1967 at Edwards AFB, California. A period of ground assessment followed, before the airframe was stored at Edwards. With no likelihood of any further flight activity, the aircraft was allocated to the Air Force Flight Test Museum at the base.

The F-111 was still being evaluated when the first examples visited Europe. In May 1967, F-111As 65-5701 and 65-5702 flew non-stop, without aerial refuelling from the USA to RAF Wethersfield, UK to permit the 20th Tactical Fighter Wing (TFW) to view its anticipated future equipment. At the time, the Wing was flying the North American F-100 Super Sabre, which was performing sterling service in

F-111A 63-9769 in an unusual natural metal finish. The extension to the rear of the fuselage is a parachute pack to evaluate spinning techniques. (GD)

Pre-production F-111A 65-7701 being towed prior to departing RAF Wethersfield for the Paris Air Show in May 1967. The Wethersfield visit enabled 20th TFW personnel to view their future equipment. (via Lindsay Peacock)

Vietnam in the fighter-bomber, CAS role. However, against the formidable Warsaw Pact, the Sled, as the F-100 was known, did not really stand a chance! The three squadrons assigned to the Wing were the 55th and 77th Tactical Fighter Squadrons (TFS), located at Wethersfield, while the 79th TFS was stationed at Woodbridge. Neither base was considered suitable for the new F-111, as both locations were inadequate for three fighter-bomber squadrons, lacking the infrastructure to house weapons, support and family accommodation. Therefore, the decision to re-equip the Wing with the F-111 was only possible once the unit relocated to Upper Heyford. The latter was a giant facility, with everything needed upon which to build the necessary support for the new resource.

The May 1967 flight to the UK was the first occasion that a fighter-type aircraft had made a trans-Atlantic crossing without aerial refuelling. The two F-111As were on their way to participate at the Paris Air Show, enabling potential customers and NATO officials to view the latest technology. At the completion of the event, the two pre-production F-111As returned to their development programme. Having been tantalised by the prospect of Mach 2, swing-wing and a terrain-following capability, the Wing began to prepare for delivery of the F-111 and transfer the F-100s to the Air National Guard.

However, prior to assuming responsibility for Upper Heyford, the 20th TFW had to await Strategic Air Command's (SAC) relocation of its northern European reconnaissance operation. SAC had only arrived at Upper Heyford from Brize Norton early in 1965, so was none too happy to be on the move again so soon. While the small numbers of deployed Boeing RC-135s and their support KC-135A

GD sponsored two F-111As, including 65-5702 as the first of the type to visit Europe in May 1967. The F-111 is in the static display at Le Bourget for the Paris Air Show. The large red number 179 is the Paris Air Show number. (Geoff Peck)

Stratotankers could be moved with comparative ease, it was the large support organisation, with its inherent layers of security, which was the primary stumbling block. Furthermore, SAC was in the process of introducing the new Big Team RC-135s into service, having only just retired the Boeing RB-47 Stratojets. Therefore, the Command needed a period of stability to carry out this major replacement programme, before concentrating on another move.

Mildenhall had been the primary 'bolt-hole' for the UK strategic reconnaissance operation when Upper Heyford had runway work or was closed for other reasons such as poor weather. Therefore, SAC began to prepare Mildenhall to be its new base. In the interim, France had withdrawn from NATO and expelled all overseas forces from its territory. Amongst these was the 66th Tactical Reconnaissance Wing which relocated from Laon Air Base to Upper Heyford with two squadrons of McDonnell RF-101C Voodoos, officially arriving on 10 August 1966. The latter move was the first return of fighter-sized aircraft to Upper Heyford for almost two decades, as the base had previously been occupied by the RAF for training during World War Two.

With the introduction of the first F-111As into operational service, US Air Forces in Europe began to highlight the need for a tactical fighter-bomber with the capability to operate effectively in all weather and at night. The F-111E was seen as the ideal version to be stationed within their theatre. The F-111E model had already begun deliveries to the 27th TFW at Cannon AFB, New Mexico, with the initial aircraft arriving on 20 August 1969. Almost 30 aircraft were assigned by year end, when yet another F-111A loss caused a grounding order to be imposed. Following rectification, the aircraft resumed flight operations in July 1970, with the 27th TFW beginning to make arrangements for the

The GD facility towards the end of the 1960s with some 60 to 70 F-111s parked on various aprons awaiting delivery. (GD)

transfer of the version to the UK. Before officially relocating to Upper Heyford on 1 December 1969, the 20th TFW began to send its F-100s back to the USA, with only a handful of Super Sabres actually resident at the new base. The last F-100 departed during February 1971.

Backbone of European Deterrence

During the 1980s, there were suggestions that the Soviet military feared the F-111 more than any other tactical weapons system in USAFE service at the time. Aircrew believed this to be the case and created a patch worn on their flight suits, declaring 'The F-111 – Warsaw Pact Central Heating'. Personnel associated with the F-111 were supremely confident that they could carry out their assigned mission and return to safety without significant losses. For a quarter of a century, encompassing almost half of the Cold War period, some 170 F-111s faced a redoubtable foe across a divided Europe. The combination of speed and low altitude, guided by an effective terrain-following radar (TFR), enabled delivery of a wide variety of formidable weapons systems, both conventional and nuclear, affording the US with a first-class platform!

The GD F-111 Aardvark and EF-111A Raven were stationed at various facilities across the USA, as well as Europe. In the UK, both versions were a familiar sight, especially within designated low-level corridors.

The two early combat operations in Vietnam were followed by a lengthy gap before the F-111 was involved in conflict again. Operations *El Dorado Canyon* and *Desert Storm* proved the worth of the system – the latter campaign lasting only six weeks, but nevertheless it resulted in an extensive

Left: 48th TFW F-111F 70-2415 formates with Wisconsin ANG KC-135E 57-2604 over the North Sea. The aircraft was a participant in both *El Dorado Canyon* and *Desert Storm*. (USAF)

Below: 20th TFW commander's aircraft, 67-0120 over the North Sea in July 1992. The multicoloured tail flash has been a feature since at least the F-100 Super Sabre era of the late 1950s. (T Malcolm English)

A Shaky Beginning

combat tally. Many of the participating aircraft displayed mission symbols on the nose, applied by their respective crew chief very soon after each had received post-flight preparations. However, no aircraft type remains operational forever, and despite this success, all examples of the USAF F-111s had been retired by the end of the 1990s – their operations and colour schemes now consigned to history. Australia followed suit by the end of 2010.

The F-111 was an amazing aircraft that was capable of delivering many sophisticated weapons with pinpoint accuracy. While day-to-day training sorties were conducted from their home bases, with small practice munitions, or simulation of larger ordnance, regular deployments to facilities to utilise live firing ranges, particularly in Europe, enabled aircrews to familiarise themselves with other armaments. Apart from these training missions, F-111s were flown across Europe to enable crews to practise routes to be flown in the event of hostilities. Therefore, the F-111 was a commonplace asset within the USAFE theatre of operations.

The Sacramento Air Materiel Area (later Air Logistics Center (ALC)) at McClellan AFB, California, was the primary overhaul facility for all versions of the F-111. Air Force Logistics Command, and from 1 July 1992, Air Force Materiel Command, was responsible for this and other centres. The Sacramento ALC had a small number of F-111s assigned for test duties, consisting of at least one example of each version produced. The 2874th Test Squadron was activated on 15 January 1988 for this purpose, which was replaced by the 337th Test Squadron on 2 October 1992. Tail code 'SM' was applied to some aircraft, while others were flown with the Sacramento ALC triangular logo on the tail.

Named *The Chief*, for the 20th wing CO, and parked at Upper Heyford after a rain shower. (Stu Freer)

68-0175 is one of a small number of F-111s operated by the Sacramento Air Logistics Center (SMALC), at McClellan AFB. The SMALC had a mix of versions, primarily to evaluate upgrades as well as offering assigned test pilots with the opportunity to maintain proficiency. Seen visiting Nellis AFB in February 1981. Note the SMALC F-111 emblem on the fuselage. (Bill Peake)

Chapter 2
The F-111A

As stated, the initial production version was the F-111A, which was first ordered in 1966. The technology incorporated offered the Air Force a quantum leap forward in capability. The first two aircraft from the fiscal year 1966 order were also utilised for development, while the remaining 129 were assigned to operational duties. Initial production airframes performed the training role, with the remainder carrying out operational flying to bring crews up to full combat-ready status.

Initial plans were for operational deliveries to begin on 16 October 1967 to the 474th TFW at Cannon AFB, New Mexico, for the 428th TFS. However, the squadron was not operational at the time, and remained so in 'paper status' only, until relocated to Nellis AFB on 20 January 1968. Therefore, it is unlikely any F-111As were actually delivered to Cannon AFB. The Wing also relocated to Nellis AFB, Nevada, on 20 January 1968, gaining responsibility for the 4527th Combat Crew Training Squadron, which formed on the same day. The first three aircraft, serials 66-0013, 66-0014 and 66-0015, all joined the new training unit. The 428th TFS also began receiving new F-111As around the same time, reaching initial operating capability on 28 April 1968.

Left: Pre-production F-111A 63-9772 armed with inert 750lb M117 bombs during weapons evaluation tests. Unusually they are attached to multiple ejection racks rather than underwing hard points. At the completion of development tasks, the aircraft was used for ground training with the Sheppard Technical Training Center (TTC). (Lockheed Martin)

Below: F-111A 67-0114 with tail code 'NC' of the 430th TFS. Large tail stripes were in vogue during April 1970 when the image was taken. (Tom Brewer)

F-111A 66-0023 wearing the squadron allocated tail code 'WF' of the 4539th Fighter Weapons Squadron at Nellis AFB during May 1968. (via Steve Hill)

Nellis was an ideal location, as the nearby ranges afforded almost unlimited flying opportunities at all levels, enabling aircrew the airspace required to practise the new capabilities. Coincidentally, the simplified (by comparison) McDonnell F-4 Phantom was also entering service at the same time, but, seemingly, enjoying a much less complicated introduction. However, sources claim the troublesome F-111 could deliver several times the bomb load of an F-4, offering an obvious increase in potential. Depending on the type of ordnance attached, the F-111 could carry two and, some say, even three times the load of a Phantom.

Apart from the 474th, F-111s were also delivered to the 4539th Fighter Weapons Squadron, 4525th Fighter Weapons Wing (FWW), at Nellis, whose primary duty was to develop operational tactics, including weapons delivery. The Red Flag school had yet to be devised, with USAF crews learning limited strategy at their home stations, resulting in fighter aircraft succumbing to North Vietnamese air defences almost on a daily basis. The adage 'you train as you fight' was not yet on the curriculum, resulting in combat operations being a wake-up call to many pilots. The North Vietnamese tactics were simply to prevent fighter-bomber missions from delivering their ordnance on their targets, with ground-to-air defences being widespread and extremely effective. Air-to-air combat by the MiG-21s was a close second. However, it was not until November 1973 that the first Red Flag courses began, offering crews the opportunity to experience realistic training, by simulating scenarios that were likely to be encountered. But, this was too late for F-111 crews deployed to South East Asia (SEA).

F-111A Combat Debut

The Air Force was eager to employ the new F-111A in combat operations in Vietnam. The combination of a night, all-weather capability, with the TFR system seemed ideal for well defended tactical targets in the north. In preparation to begin combat, the Air Force conducted Exercise Combat Bullseye I early in 1967, using development aircraft, including 65-5704, to determine if the F-111 was ready to deploy. This was followed by a further evaluation, called Harvest Reaper in June 1967, which addressed shortcomings in relation to night and all-weather capabilities. These preparations preceded the deployment of six 474th TFW aircraft to Takhli RTAFB, Thailand, under Operation *Combat Lancer*, arriving on 17 March 1968. Detachment 1, 428th TFS, was formed to operate the aircraft while deployed.

Due to ill-advised haste, the aircraft began combat missions immediately, performing a strike against a North Vietnamese storage area and truck park some hours after arriving in Thailand. Other missions followed, but so did losses. F-111A 66-0022 was tasked with a mission against a target north of the Demilitarized Zone near Chanh Hoa on 28 March 1968. However, the aircraft failed to return,

The 22nd F-111A 65-5704 wearing the Air Force Systems Command emblem on the fuselage side. Evaluated during *Harvest Reaper* in 1967 to determine combat performance ahead of the *Combat Lancer* deployment. Shortly after arriving for storage at MASDC on 11 March 1971. (Roy Lock)

F-111A 66-0018 with the small *Harvest Reaper* markings on the rudder. At Nellis AFB shortly after the detachment had returned from Thailand. (Ray Leader)

with neither the crew nor wreckage ever being located. Speculation was that the F-111 suffered a malfunction, flew into the ground or was brought down by enemy fire. Whatever the reason, it was a major setback to the operation.

Two days later, control was lost by F-111A 66-0017 while over Thailand, with the crew ejecting using the cockpit capsule. The cause was a simple solidified sealant, which blocked the pitch/roll assembly causing the stabiliser mechanism to jam. On 22 April 1968, F-111A 66-0024 was on a low-level strike against a ferry at Phoung Chay over the Xe Lanong River in Laos when it disappeared. Again, speculation was that the aircraft flew into the ground, despite the North Vietnamese claiming to have brought the F-111 down with ground fire. Subsequently, all F-111 combat operations were suspended, although crews continued to fly local training sorties until 22 November 1968 when the decision was made to end the detachment and return to the USA. Only 55 combat sorties were flown, which for the loss of three aircraft and two crews was hardly a promising start to the F-111's career.

Four years passed before the Air Force elected to return F-111s to SEA. The North Vietnamese Spring Offensive in 1972 followed the familiar pattern of a major invasion, boosted by the perceived ineffectiveness of the South Vietnamese military and the earlier gradual withdrawal of some US forces from the region. With these two factors appearing to be in their favour, the North hoped to swiftly overrun the South, although the plan was hampered by the US swiftly bolstering combat

Above left: F-111A 67-0087 of 347th TFW refuelling from a KC-135 during a training mission over Thailand. The yellow stripe code is for the 429th TFS. (Adrian Balch collection)

Above right: F-111A 67-0098 at Takhli RTAFB, Thailand, shortly after arriving in September 1972. (via Chris Knott)

aircraft strength in the region. One of the last elements to be deployed were F-111As from the 474th TFW, which, at the time, was considered to be the most combat ready tactical unit. All three Nellis-based squadrons contributed, with a total of 48 F-111As deployed to Takhli RTAFB, beginning on 27 September 1972, joining the hastily organised 474th TFW (Advanced Echelon). They were reassigned to the 347th TFW from 30 July 1973 and moved to Korat RTAFB on 12 July 1974. The operation ended in mid-June 1975, with the aircraft returning home.

The increase of additional US assets in the SEA theatre was conducted under a series of operations entitled *Constant Guard*, with one group of F-111As flown direct from Nellis AFB to Thailand. Once in theatre, some aircraft were prepared for their first combat mission, which was carried out just 33 hours after leaving the USA! Nevertheless, the initial combat loss was suffered on the first evening, when F-111A 67-0078 was destroyed near the target over Laos. For the third time, the circumstances of the loss were the subject of conjecture. Theories ranged from being shot down, flying into the ground or being destroyed by its own Mark 84 bombs, struck by shrapnel from the exploding munitions.

The second combat loss involved 67-0066 which crashed while attacking a railway bridge near Dia Loi on 16 October 1972. The cause of the disappearance was undetermined and could also have been related to Mark 84 bombs. Soon afterwards, on 7 November 1972, 67-0063 was brought down by ground fire while attacking a ferry crossing at Luat Son in southern Laos. The commencement of Operation *Linebacker II* on 18 December 1972 resulted in only one aircraft loss on the first evening, with F-111A 67-0099 going missing while attacking the main radio communications transmitter in Hanoi. The aircraft successfully bombed the target but reportedly crashed into the sea afterwards. On the evening of 22 December 1972, F-111A 67-0068 was brought down by ground fire while on a strike mission against a target on the Red River in the suburbs of Hanoi.

Two more F-111As were lost during the SEA campaign, although neither were combat related. The first was 67-0072 which suffered the main undercarriage collapsing on take-off from Takhli RTAFB on 21 February 1973. Flames soon spread to the full load of Mark 82 bombs, which exploded periodically, preventing the fire department from tackling the inferno for many hours. The final accident involved 77-0111 which collided with 77-0094 near Takhli on 16 June 1973. The former became uncontrollable, forcing the crew to eject. The second aircraft lost a sizeable chunk of wing but managed to make an emergency landing at Udorn RTAFB.

The deployment was considerably more successful than the 1968 visit. During the intervening four years, many of the deficiencies had been rectified. In addition, crews had become far more proficient at understanding the complex systems which were incorporated. Eight aircraft were lost to enemy action or accidents, although this was quite minimal, considering the vast number of combat sorties flown. Combat operations were mostly performed at night as single ship sorties, at very low level. During *Linebacker II*, for example, single F-111s flew more than 140 missions, achieving impressive bomb damage estimation. Indeed, such was the effect of the combined operation that the North Vietnamese representatives agreed to resume peace negotiations. The accuracy of F-111 sorties had a sufficiently compelling impact on North Vietnamese targets that there was no choice but for talks to recommence.

Mayaguez Incident

During May 1975, forces of the Khmer Rouge seized the container ship SS *Mayaguez*, which was sailing through Kampuchean waters. A pair of 347th TFW F-111As were tasked to search for the vessel. The ship was soon located, with a number of US Marines boarding, although the crew had been removed to a nearby island. During an attempted rescue, the Marines encountered fierce resistance. Aviation involvement was mostly confined to the Marines, although an F-111A detected and sank a hostile Khmer Rouge patrol boat escorting the seized ship. This was one of the final acts for the F-111As in SEA, as the aircraft returned to the USA the following month. The F-111As rejoined the 474th TFW at Nellis, although it is believed that no aircraft were decorated with any combat markings beneath the cockpit.

As will be readily apparent, the two sets of deployments saw three aircraft lost in 1968, with a further eight in the 1972–73 period. Despite an inauspicious start, the F-111 flew some 3,000 missions before the January 1973 Paris Peace Accord. This impressive tally proved to sceptics that the F-111 was an excellent fighter-bomber, validating the faith that earlier, far too few senior personnel had in the type.

The period spent flying into North Vietnam, and elsewhere in SEA, was not lost upon Cold War adversaries, China and the Soviet Union. At the time, the F-111 was the most advanced tactical warplane in the American arsenal, with the North Vietnamese quick to gather fragments of destroyed F-111s to pass to their financial backers. It is highly likely that sufficient components were passed to

F-111A 67-0081 coded 'HG' of 347th TFW at Nellis, shortly after the aircraft departed from Korat RTAFB, Thailand, in June 1975. The aircraft reverted to the 474th TFW and was eventually recoded 'NA'. (via Steve Hill)

F-111A 66-0015 was the third operational aircraft to be delivered to the 4527th TFTS at Nellis AFB during January 1968. Later, it was with the 428th TFS and was eventually converted to an EF-111A. (Adrian Balch collection)

F-111A 67-0076 painted in special bicentennial colours at Nellis AFB in July 1976. (Don Logan)

Beijing and Moscow for indigenous aerospace technicians to evaluate. However, neither nation reverse engineered an identical copy of the F-111 of their own, clearly pointing to the belief that the type was a complicated design, which would be difficult to replicate. The Soviets, in particular, traditionally constructed rugged designs, which the F-111 undoubtedly was not. Therefore, it is understandable that the 'opposition' was not prepared to invest time and effort into copying early 1960s technology, when on the horizon were more advanced designs with a less complicated configuration. The Russian Central Aerohydrodynamic Institute, also known as the TsAGI, at Zhukovsky is the premier laboratory where foreign aircraft and components have been evaluated for many years. It is more than likely that parts from F-111s brought down in SEA found their way to this research centre.

Operation *Ready Switch*

After ten years of F-111 service, the Air Force decided to embark upon a three-way exchange of aircraft. This involved the 474th, 366th TFW at Mountain Home AFB, Idaho, and the 48th TFW at RAF Lakenheath, UK. Designated Operation *Ready Switch*, the 474th was to transfer their F-111As to Mountain Home. In turn, the 366th would send their F-111Fs to Lakenheath, while the latter's F-4Ds would be reassigned to Nellis. In reality, the ex-Lakenheath F-4Ds joined several wings, permitting aircraft from similar block numbers and configurations to be integrated. This reshuffle of assets occurred during the second half of 1977. The relocation of the F-111F models to USAFE was a crucial step, designed to reinforce the capability of assets close to the potential Warsaw Pact frontline but stationed sufficiently to the rear of the area to maintain their safety. The presence of four squadrons of F-111Fs, in addition to the three F-111Es already in the UK, was not lost upon the Soviet Union.

The surviving F-111As remained with the 366th until June–July 1991, when they were retired to Davis-Monthan (D-M) AFB for storage. Not all F-111As served their entire career in the fighter-bomber role. Grumman, which had earlier designed the EA-6B Prowler for the Navy, won a contract to convert 42 F-111A to EF-111A configuration for the electronic warfare role – see later.

F-111A 67-0076 in formation with a pair of Republic of Korean Air Force F-4Ds, during a deployment to South Korea. Interestingly, one, and possibly both, of the F-4Ds were initially assigned to the 36th TFW at Bitburg AB, Germany before being reassigned to Korea. (USAF)

Chapter 3

The F-111B and F-111D

F-111B

As stated, the F-111 was to have been a joint Navy–Air Force project, which was guided by the deft hand of Robert McNamara who was Secretary of Defense from 1961 until 1968. He was the main advocate of both branches operating the same type of aircraft for their respective fighter roles. However, the problems associated with spiralling costs and delays eventually caused the Navy to abandon plans and instead opt for the McDonnell F-4 Phantom. Losses were also a factor in the Navy's decision. Eventually only seven F-111Bs were produced.

The first Navy F-111B was 151970, which was exhibited at Edwards AFB air show static in May 1968. This was just two months before the test programme was completed, with the aircraft withdrawn from use at the Naval Air Test Facility at Lakehurst, New Jersey. An XAIM-54A development Phoenix missile is attached to the underwing hard point. (Geoff Peck)

F-111B 151974 was ferried to Moffett Field during October 1968 for wind tunnel testing with NASA's Ames Laboratory. The aircraft was retired from flying soon afterwards and subsequently scrapped. (NASA)

One of only two Navy pre-production F-111Bs completed, 152715 parked on a range at China Lake, California during April 1989. A two-year period of evaluation preceded the aircraft being retired. (Paul Bigelow)

The first flight by an F-111B took place on 18 May 1965. Five prototypes were ordered, followed by just two pre-production versions. A further two of the latter were not completed, while two batches of production aircraft, comprising 20 and eight examples, were cancelled. The aircraft from the first of these batches would almost certainly have been assigned to the Fleet Replacement Squadron to train aircrew. The second batch was probably the complement for the initial Fleet Squadron.

Evaluation was conducted at the usual Navy facilities, including the Naval Missile Center at Point Mugu, California, the Naval Air Test Center at NAS Patuxent River, Maryland and the Naval Air Test Facility at Lakehurst, New Jersey. In addition, Grumman carried out development, on behalf of GD, from its Bethpage, New York plant. The Navy aircraft were also flown from Culver City Airport, California, where the Hughes Aircraft Company was producing the AIM-54 Phoenix missile specifically for the F-111B. Mating the weapon to the aircraft was no easy task!

The Navy programme was cancelled in 1968, with the survivors of the seven aircraft produced being retired by mid-1971. Only one was flown to the Military Aircraft Storage and Disposition Center at D-M AFB, Arizona, while two were retired to the Naval Weapons Center at China Lake, California, where one is retained, having spent many years parked outside on one of the ranges. The void left by the cancelled F-111 was subsequently filled by the F-4, and later the Grumman F-14 Tomcat. Ironically GD teamed with Grumman for development and testing of the F-111B, due to the former having no experience with carrier-borne fighters. When the Navy part of the programme was cancelled, Grumman was able to use some of the design features to create its F-14.

F-111D

Very few military aircraft types spend their entire operational career with just one unit. However, the F-111D was flown by a single wing operationally, from initial deliveries until final retirement. The 27th TFW at Cannon AFB, New Mexico, flew other versions for short periods, but the F-111D model was the mainstay of the Wing.

The F-111 was purchased in reasonable numbers, with different versions emerging as new features were developed. Although the F-111D would appear to have been in advance of the F-111E model sequentially, in reality the former was actually the third version to emerge. This was due to the F-111E model being an enhanced

F-111D 68-0127 specially marked for the 27th wing CO, alongside 68-0122 of the 522nd TFS at Cannon AFB during December 1988. The latter has a GBU-10E/B laser-guided bomb, although the F-111D model could not laser-designate. Instead, crews practised with special forces using ground-based lasers to designate. (Henk Schuitemaker)

Left: Another test aircraft, F-111D 68-0089 displaying tail code 'ED' departing Edwards AFB in March 1985. The aircraft spent its entire 19 years of service on test duties at Edwards. (Photographer unknown)

Below: Unusual serial presentation on 27th TFW F-111D 68-0111, displayed as AF68-111D, with the appropriate black letters/numbers highlighted in white to spell out F111D. At Nellis AFB in April 1989. (Kirk Minert)

Named *City of Clovis* on the nose-wheel door, 27th TFW commander's F-111D 68-0127 at George AFB, California, in November 1990. With a quartet of squadrons assigned at the time, the fin tip has all four colours displayed. (Bob Archer)

version of the F-111A, while the F-111D featured improved avionics and other new technology which were in a category of their own. The F-111E was fitted with analogue avionics, whereas the F-111D featured a digital system.

A total of 96 were ordered, all budgeted in 1968. The first two F-111D models, along with a few later production examples, were allocated to test and evaluation duties. The Air Force Flight Test Center at Edwards AFB operated a small number, with at least one retained until retirement.

The first operational F-111D, serial 68-0087, was delivered to Cannon AFB on 17 November 1971, joining the 4427th Tactical Fighter Replacement Squadron, 27th TFW, which had been activated six weeks earlier on 1 October. Tail code 'CE' was applied but changed to 'CC' on 1 April 1972, in accordance with order AFM66-1. Several other squadrons flew the F-111D throughout the tenure of the 27th TFW. For the majority of the time, the 27th was assigned four squadrons, consisting of the 481st, 522nd, 523rd and 524th, with various suffix designations. The last F-111D was delivered to Cannon on 28 February 1973. Each squadron had a nominal strength of 18–20 aircraft, although the training unit operated slightly more. The 4427th Tactical Fighter Reconnaissance Squadron (TFRS) was the initial training unit but was replaced by the 481st Tactical Reconnaissance Training Squadron (TFTS) in January 1976 and the 524th TFTS in January 1980.

Overseas deployments were occasionally undertaken, including at least one to the UK, another to South Korea, plus a deployment to Egypt for Exercise Bright Star. However, for the majority of the 21 years that the F-111D was active, the aircraft flew from home base, or were involved in exercises at other Tactical Air Command bases. The arrival of the F-111E, F-111F and F-111G models at Cannon enabled the F-111D model to be retired with the final pair, serials 68-0104 and 68-0134, departing on 16 December 1992 for D-M AFB. However, the ultimate F-111D model in service was 68-0175 of the 337th TS, which was retired on 28 December 1992.

Four 27th TFW F-111Ds overflying the Pyramids during a deployment to Egypt to participate in Exercise Bright Star in October 1983. (USAF)

A quartet of 27th FW commanders' F-111s, headed by a conventional camouflaged F-111D with all four colours for the wing CO, flanked by an EF-111A of the 430th ECS, an F-111G and an F-111F of the 428th and 524th FSs. (USAF photo)

Chapter 4

The F-111E

The F-111E was an upgraded version of the F-111A, which retained the older avionics suite, but featured an improved weapons delivery capability, as well as engine operation enhancements. Ninety-four F-111E-models were produced, with the first joining the 27th TFW on 20 August 1969, due to delays with the planned F-111D model. The 27th flew the F-111E until March 1971, when the aircraft were grounded. After the order was rescinded, the Air Force implemented the plan to bolster USAFE by stationing the F-111E in the UK, enabling the 27th finally to convert to the F-111D.

Above: F-111E 68-0014 of the 77th TFS taxiing at Upper Heyford during September 1979 with white tail code and serial. (Paul Bennett)

Right: Close-up of an Indian chief's head and nose inscription *The Chief* on F-111E 68-0020 during September 1991. (Bob Archer)

The Chief, 68-0020 taking off from Upper Heyford in December 1993 for the last time, to end operations at the base. (Chris Lofting)

Above: 20th TFW 68-0028 wearing a special colour scheme for the bicentennial. Seen at Ramstein AB, Germany in August 1976. (via Steve Hill)

Left: Close-up of the bicentennial markings on the tail of 68-0028 at Upper Heyford in July 1976. (Bob Archer)

Above left: Prior to being christened *The Chief*, 68-0020 was named *My Lucky Blonde* at Coningsby in June 1986. (Bob Archer)

Above right: The only European-based F-111 to be repainted in a dark gunship grey scheme was 68-0050 of the 20th TFW seen landing at Upper Heyford circa 1990. (Kevin Wills)

The first F-111Es arrived at Upper Heyford in September 1970, with the Wing wasting no time in transitioning all three squadrons to operational status. As stated, the F-111E was the first of the type to be stationed in Europe. The 55th, 77th and 79th TFSs planned to allocate tail codes 'US', 'UT' and 'UR' respectively, although only the last was physically applied. The use of code 'US' by the F-111 was considered inappropriate, as this could be seen as indicating the type was 'unserviceable'. However, the Wing did not have the opportunity to use 'UT', as in January 1971, the 55th, 77th and 79th were reallocated tail codes 'JS', 'JT' and 'JR' respectively. All three codes were carried until 1 April 1972 when the Department of the Air Force issued directive AFM66-1, which ordered tail codes to be changed from allocation at squadron to wing level. Prior to AFM66-1, USAFE had adopted a set sequence, with the second letter for each wing being R, S, T and so forth. However, the Air Force was happy to permit the 20th to adopt a tail code outside of this framework on condition that it was not already in use. As tail code 'UH', indicating Upper Heyford, was available, the 20th changed to this two-letter identifier, which was retained until the wing returned home at the end of the Cold War.

The majority of operations involved training exercises at home station, as well as regular squadron-level deployments to use the bombing ranges near Zaragoza, Spain and Incirlik, Turkey. Apart from enjoying better weather than the UK (Upper Heyford was reported to endure the second worst weather conditions within USAFE – with Hahn Air Base, Germany, apparently, occupying the number one spot), Spain and Turkey have less congested airspace. The two ranges are located in areas with very little conflicting air traffic, ensuring the F-111s had the opportunity to deliver live ordnance while flying at low level, thereby familiarising crews with the TFR system.

Interestingly, during 1976, under the tenure of President Jimmy Carter, much of the budget for spare parts for military hardware was redirected to social programmes. The 20th TFW was affected quite badly, with mission capable rates (MCR) falling to below 50 per cent, and with aircraft being cannibalised for parts to try and maintain a reasonable state of readiness. This was at a time when the USSR was increasing preparedness and amassing larger concentrations of forces along the NATO–Warsaw Pact border. Indeed, many in senior NATO positions believed the chances of a conventional war with the USSR in Europe during 1980 to be 50/50. However, the election of President Ronald Reagan addressed the problem, and by 1982 MCRs were improving significantly.

The 42nd Electronic Combat Squadron (ECS) was formed at Upper Heyford in July 1983 to operate the EF-111A, although the first Raven was not delivered until 3 February 1984. With deliveries being much slower than anticipated, the squadron was allocated eight F-111Es to enable aircrew to remain current. These began to join the squadron in March 1984 and remained operational until 1 July 1985 when the unit was transferred to the 66th Electronic Combat Wing (ECW).

Interestingly, F-111E 68-0050 was reported to have been badly damaged inside a hardened aircraft shelter at Upper Heyford during spring 1986 when a liquid oxygen bottle exploded. The eruption almost

68-0055 taxiing at Upper Heyford in August 1993. (Ray Sumner)

severed the aircraft in two. After being dismantled, the aircraft was believed to have departed for Fort Worth inside 63rd MAW C-141B 66-0138 on 11 September 1986. The lengthy rebuild was completed by 30 March 1989, when 68-0050 flew to McClellan AFB to become the pattern aircraft for the Avionics Modernisation Program (AMP). Additionally, the Vietnam-style camouflage had been replaced by the gunship grey scheme – the only USAFE F-111 to receive this design. Having satisfactorily completed evaluation with the SMALC, the F-111 was returned to the 20th TFW on 31 January 1990.

A further 24 additional F-111Es received the AMP update, with all being converted by BAE Systems at their Bristol Filton facility. Whereas the unmodified aircraft were retired when the 20th relinquished the F-111E, the AMP airframes continued in service with the 27th Fighter Wing (FW).

Operation *Ghost Rider*

The F-111E was not considered for Operation *El Dorado Canyon*, the bombing raid on Libyan targets in April 1986. This was because the version lacked the Ford Aerospace AN/AVQ-26 PAVE Tack laser target acquisition system, which was fitted to the F-111F. However, the 20th TFW was involved in an evaluation of the tactics likely to be used in a long-range air strike. The Wing was notified of the highly classified Operation *Ghost Rider*, which would involve ten F-111Es, each armed with eight Mark 82 500lb inert bombs. The mission was to fly six hours non-stop to a range located southwest of Goose

F-111E 68-0052, with a blue dice showing the number five, over the North Sea during an aerial refuelling mission in July 1992. The aircraft crashed into the approach lights at Upper Heyford on 17 September 1992. (T Malcolm English)

Bay, Canada, with the assistance of KC-135s launched from Mildenhall. The ten primary aircraft and four air spares, manned by highly experienced aircrew, launched at 0425hrs local time on the morning of 18 October 1985 and met with seven KC-135s. The ten aircraft dropped their ordnance within the precise 'time on target', before turning east and returning to Upper Heyford. The objective was to destroy simulated runways. The operation was considered a success, with procedures for planning and executing the mission incorporated into the organisation subsequently for *El Dorado Canyon*.

Operation *Proven Force*

Despite the F-111E not being included in the Libyan operation, the version did not bow out of service without proving itself in combat. The 79th TFS was on weapons training deployment at Incirlik AB, Turkey when the Iraqis invaded Kuwait in early August 1990. The squadron carried on as normal and returned to Upper Heyford by 13 August. The 77th deployed east with 14 aircraft, arriving by 9 August. Despite having completed their planned cycle, their aircraft and personnel remained as the unit began concentrating on preparation for combat. The 7440th Provisional Wing was formed at Incirlik, with elements drawn mostly from USAFE units. Subsequently the 79th TFS assumed responsibility for the deployed F-111Es but was augmented by personnel and aircraft from the other two squadrons of the 20th TFW. Approximately 24 F-111Es were in theatre throughout the build-up of forces during the latter months of 1990. When *Desert Storm* began on 17 January, the F-111Es were tasked with Iraqi targets north of Baghdad, being flown under Operation *Proven Force*.

During the early hours of 18 January, a dozen F-111Es departed Incirlik as the primary strike element supported by defence suppression F-16CJs and electronic jamming from EC-130H and EF-111As, plus other assets. As the F-111Es were not fitted with the PAVE Tack laser targeting system, crews were required to identify targets by radar. Missions were initially flown at extremely low level, around 200 feet, using the TFR, but due to intensive anti-aircraft fire, the tactics were quickly revised. Instead, sorties were flown at low, medium and high level, depending on the target and ground defences. At least one pilot wryly joked that the Iraqi triple-A was so intense and bright that it was almost possible to read maps by it.

Above left: F-111E 67-0121 with 21 bomb symbols from combat sorties over Northern Iraq during *Proven Force* early in 1991. (Bob Archer)

Above right: 79th Fighter Squadron F-111E 68-0013 displaying 24 mission marks while operating from Incirlik AB during Operation *Proven Force*. Photographed in July 1991. (Bob Archer)

 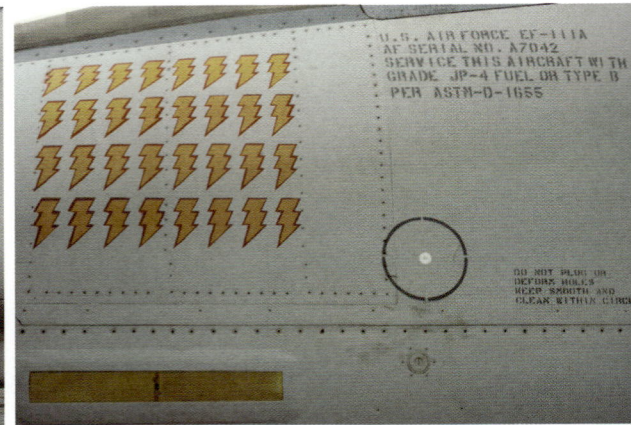

Above left: 42nd ECS EF-111A 67-0042 at Fairford in July 1992 displaying 32 Proven Force combat mission marks. Yet another with the familiar crow reference, this one being *The Old Crow*. (Bob Archer)

Above right: Close-up of the 32 lightning flashes applied following participation in Operation *Proven Force* at Incirlik AB, Turkey. Seventeen months after being applied, the mission markings were still displayed. (Bob Archer)

The F-111s flew almost every day, gradually taking out targets across their area of operations. A total of 470 sorties were flown, striking 423 targets and accumulating 1,350 combat hours. Due to Incirlik Air Base being quite close to the Iraqi border, some sorties were accomplished without aerial refuelling, although tanker support was available whenever *Proven Force* strike packages were airborne. The majority of aircraft returned to Upper Heyford on 9 March 1991, comprising 22 F-111Es, together with five EF-111As.

However, with Saddam Hussein remaining in place and in charge of the central region of Iraq, there was a requirement to impose the United Nations air exclusion zone. The Iraqis periodically flew hostile missions, although on most occasions they returned to their home station as soon as fighter aircraft attempted an intercept. F-111Es and EF-111As were included in the composition of the mixed complement which was deployed to the region on a rotational basis for Operation *Provide Comfort*.

20th FW F-111E 68-0061 *Last Roll of the Dice*, wearing a full colour wing emblem on the fin, and 68-0055 *Heartbreaker*, shortly before taxiing out to return to the USA. The departure on 7 December 1993 ended F-111s at Upper Heyford. (Darron Hall)

The F-111E

Above left: *Last Roll of the Dice* artwork depicts a P-38 linking to an F-111 in afterburner, on the nose of 68-0061. At Upper Heyford in December 1993. (Darron Hall)

Above right: 68-0061 lifts off from Upper Heyford for the last time on 7 December 1993. This, and the other pair, ended 20th FW F-111 operations in Europe. (Chris Lofting)

Right: Close-up of the nose art and *Heartbreaker* inscription on F-111E 68-0055. At Upper Heyford in December 1993, shortly before departing for the USA for display at Robins AFB, Georgia. (Darron Hall)

Coincidentally, as the Middle East campaign was escalating, so the Cold War was receding. The peace dividend between the two old adversaries offered the opportunity for a large-scale reduction in the number of squadrons assigned to the USAF. The 20th was one such unit, with the F-111Es returning home, beginning on 8 May 1992. F-111E 68-0009 initiated the process when departing for D-M AFB, with a stopover at Plattsburgh AFB, New York. Others followed at regular intervals. The final three examples departed on 7 December 1993, serials 68-0020, with special marks for the wing CO and named *The Chief*, 68-0055 with marks for the 55th FS CO and named *Heartbreaker* and 68-0061 named *Last Roll of the Dice*. Almost a quarter of a century of F-111E operations at Upper Heyford were commemorated with several other aircraft receiving nose art and inscriptions. The majority of aircraft were flown to D-M AFB for storage and eventual disposal. However, despite the retirement process, prior to departure, the F-111Es continued to perform routine sorties. F-111E 68-0064 received the large nose inscription '6,000 GENERAL DYNAMICS F111E HIGH FLYER' on 22 April 1993, having accumulated that number of flight hours earlier that day.

While the bulk of 20th F-111Es were retired from service, 24 AMP-modified aircraft were reassigned to the 428th FS in the training role, beginning in December 1992. These were assigned for just three years, until the squadron was inactivated on 12 October 1995. Despite the squadron having ceased operations, the final F-111Es did not reach D-M AFB for storage until 19 December.

20th FW F-111E 68-0064 with '6,000 GENERAL DYNAMICS F111E HIGH FLYER' to denote the first Aardvark to achieve this flying hours milestone. At Fairford in July 1993. (Bob Archer)

Left: Close-up of the unique inscription on F-111E 86-0064. (Photographer unknown)

Below: Rarely do the unsung heroes of a squadron, the maintenance personnel, receive much recognition. To rectify this omission, the sixty plus maintainers are pictured with the 55th FS F-111E 68-0055 during 1992. (USAFE)

F-111E 68-0058 of the Armament, Development and Test Center at Eglin AFB, Florida, during October 1978. The aircraft has traces of its former operator with the unit emblem of the 57th FWW on the forward fuselage, TAC badge on the tail, and 'WA' tail code, all over painted. (Paul Goddard)

Former 20th FW F-111E 68-0076 served the 428th FS at Cannon AFB four years before being retired to AMARC on 15 December 1995. Seen at Nellis AFB eight months earlier while participating in the massive Long Shot one-day exercise. (Bob Archer)

Chapter 5

The F-111F

The F-111F model was the last new version and was the most advanced, incorporating improvements which had been developed as earlier types had carried out their day-to-day operations. Some of the enhancements were simplified features, thereby reducing maintenance. The Air Force had expected to receive three Wings of F-111Ds but that was later reduced to one, with the other two planned to be equipped with the F-111F. However, this arrangement was also changed, with just the 347th TFW at Mountain Home AFB, Idaho, receiving this version when deliveries commenced on 20 September 1971. The Wing was due to receive 82 aircraft, with 58 ordered in 1970 and the final 24 the following year. However, the fiscal year 1971 order was halved. Despite the cancellation, the US congress, no doubt urged by the powerful Texan lobby, elected to fund continued production, with a dozen aircraft ordered each year from 1972 to 1975. The last 12 were also cancelled, as the Department of Defence was reluctant to budget for aircraft which the Air Force simply did not want. Nevertheless 106 F-111Fs were built, which was 24 more than originally sought. The involvement by congress to increase production, created a problem for the Air Force, which was forced to activate a fourth squadron, with all the additional operating costs.

In the interim, the 366th TFW replaced the 347th on 31 October 1972. Shortly before relocating to the UK, 19 F-111Fs were deployed at just 12 hours' notice to Taegu AB, South Korea, departing on 16 August 1976. The aircraft were deployed in response to the 'Tree Chopping Incident', under Operation *Paul Bunyan*, following a confrontation involving North Korean troops who murdered a

To commemorate the 30th anniversary of the formation of TAC, F-111F 70-2366 of the 366th TFW was decorated with full colour wing and squadron emblems, along with red, white and blue artwork on the air intake and fin tip. The milestone coincided with the 1976 bicentennial. (USAF)

70-2389 at Mountain Home AFB, Idaho, with the 366th TFW in October 1975. Two years later, the F-111Fs were reassigned from TAC to USAFE when they were transferred to the 48th TFW. (Bob Archer)

Eight F-111Fs of the 366th TFW, 390th TFS on the flight line at Mountain Home AFB in October 1975. All eight were subsequently transferred to the 48th TFW. (Bob Archer)

US Army officer in the Demilitarized Zone. United Nations officials were monitoring South Korean workers, who were supported by US troops as the lumberjacks attempted to fell an 80-foot Normandy poplar tree, which was obscuring a vital checkpoint. The North Koreans claimed the tree was planted by leader Kim Il Sung. With the possibility of the incident escalating into a full-scale conflict, the US chose to bolster assets in South Korea, including the F-111Fs, as a show of force. Subsequently, the tree was trimmed, and despite sabre rattling by the North, the situation slowly returned to normal, enabling the F-111s to return to the USA on 19 September.

As stated, the F-111F was considered to be ideal for operations in Europe, with the 48th TFW identified to transition to the new aircraft. The first three examples arrived at Lakenheath on 1 March 1977, with deliveries continuing until the final aircraft arrived in the UK on 11 November. Whereas the three

To commemorate the 40th anniversary of the original formation of the 48th Bombardment Group (Light), F-111F 71-0891 was christened *East Anglia* on 4 July 1981. A public open day coincided with a massive firework display, including two mock-up tanks firing jets of flame at one another. (Bob Archer)

72-1448 was the aircraft assigned to the 48th TFW wing CO for many years. Named *Miss Liberty* during May 1986 when the Wing was commanded by Col Sam Westbrook. (Bob Archer)

Above left: Second *Miss Liberty*, F-111F 70-2416 during May 1987. Note the aircraft is still marked with a small white bomb some 13 months after participating in *El Dorado Canyon*. (Bob Archer)

Above right: Three months before going to war, *Miss Liberty II*, F-111F 70-2390, the aircraft inscribed for 48th TFW commander Colonel Tom Lennon, at Mildenhall in May 1990. (Bob Archer)

operational F-4 squadrons at Lakenheath flew from the long-established aprons located on the southern/eastern side of the air station, the 495th TFS was activated as the fourth squadron, which primarily operated in the aircrew transition role and was situated on the north side of the facility.

Operation *El Dorado Canyon*

Support for anti-American terrorist groups was sponsored by several Arabic leaders, with Colonel Muammar Gaddafi of Libya being at the forefront. He openly financed these groups and made no secret of his assistance whenever these factions struck at defenceless targets. President Ronald Reagan, backed by UK Prime Minister Margaret Thatcher, chose to carry out an air strike to silence the vociferous colonel.

A contingency plan was formulated whereby a mixed force of US Navy carrier-borne fighters would attack one set of targets while USAF fighter-bombers would strike elsewhere in Libya. Strategic reconnaissance assets were deployed to the Mediterranean, including a pair of 17th RW TR-1As and at least two additional RC-135s. The gradual build-up of sizeable numbers of McDonnell Douglas KC-10A Extenders and KC-135s to Fairford and Mildenhall was a more obvious sign that a strike against Libya was imminent. At Fairford were eight KC-10s, along with ten KC-135s, while a further 15 KC-10s were at Mildenhall together with 20 KC-135s.

All transient air traffic at both bases was halted as personnel readied the tankers for their mission. Furthermore, most training flights at Lakenheath and Upper Heyford ceased as aircraft were armed and maintained ready for the raid. The presidential directive was issued on 14 April 1986, with tankers beginning to depart shortly after darkness fell. In customary fashion, the French and Spanish refused the armed aircraft permission to overfly their territory, so instead the fighter-bombers and their tanker support were forced to fly out over the eastern Atlantic Ocean to enter the Mediterranean Sea through the Straits of Gibraltar. The KC-10s positioned themselves in racetracks west of Portugal, with their endurance extended through aerial refuelling by the KC-135s.

At the same time as the tankers were departing, the 48th TFW began launching four cells of six aircraft each, drawn from all four squadrons. Among these were air spares, which began returning to Lakenheath once the main strike packages were safely on their way. Five EF-111A of the 42nd ECS launched from Upper Heyford around the same time, consisting of four mission aircraft and an air spare. The US Navy contingent was flown from the aircraft carriers CV-43/USS *Coral Sea* and CV-66/USS *America*. Both vessels were off the Libyan coast.

The two dozen F-111s met with their tankers at predetermined racetracks off the Iberian Peninsula and refuelled in radio silence. Once in the Mediterranean area, the USAF contingent flew well to the north of the African coast, to avoid detection and to maintain the element of surprise. The EF-111As commenced jamming radars and other Libyan air defences as the strike elements initiated their attacks. The Navy contingent was tasked with striking targets in the Benghazi area, while the USAF was assigned various objectives in Tripoli. In a matter of minutes, barracks, training areas as well as both airports were attacked. Ordnance used included 2,000lb laser-guided bombs, and 500lb high drag gravity bombs by the F-111s, whereas HARM and Shrike missiles were fired at air defence radars by the Navy aircraft.

While the Navy fighters all returned safely to their aircraft carriers, the USAF did not fare so well, with F-111F 70-2389 being lost. Some reports implied the aircraft flew into the sea, while others have suggested that it was hit by ground fire. The two crew were killed.

As soon as the F-111s had expended their ordnance, they climbed to altitude to meet with their tankers, and reverse the course back to the UK. The EF-111As were first to return, followed later by the F-111Fs,

Right: F-111F 70-2363 of the 492nd TFS, 48th TFW over East Anglia in July 1982. An electronic countermeasures pod is mounted beneath the rear fuselage. (Jim Rotromel)

Below: F-111F 70-2389 with white tail code and serial, as well as a full colour wing emblem, at Lakenheath in May 1980. The aircraft was lost, possibly to enemy ground fire, during Operation *El Dorado Canyon*, the attack on Tripoli, Libya on 15 April 1986. (Bob Archer)

Above left: A small white bomb symbol on 70-2416 after participating in Operation *El Dorado Canyon* to strike targets in Libya during April 1986. Subsequently, the mission mark was removed. (Bob Archer)

Above right: Tail embellished with the four squadron colours; an appropriate legend for the 48th TFW commander and the Libyan campaign banner. F-111F 70-2390 was one of at last four aircraft allocated to the wing CO. (Bob Archer)

which commenced touching down at Lakenheath at 0730hrs local time. Subsequently, the F-111 crew chiefs wished to mark their aircraft with the time-honoured tradition of a mission symbol. Some aircraft did display a small white bomb on the port side below the cockpit window. However, the Air Force decided later that it might make the aircraft a reprisal target for terrorists. Therefore, most of the bomb symbols were removed, with, instead, all 48th aircraft displaying a distinctive Libyan campaign banner applied across the tail. Despite this directive, 70-2413 was still displaying the mission marking in March 1989!

Post-strike, the two SR-71As of Detachment 4, 9th Strategic Reconnaissance Wing (SRW) were launched from Mildenhall to obtain photographs of the damage inflicted. Eventually, the details filtered through to Lakenheath, enabling participants to analyse details of the target damage.

Operation *Desert Shield/Desert Storm*

The next four years were relatively uneventful, until early August 1990 when Iraq invaded Kuwait. Soon afterwards, the 48th TFW was notified to prepare to be included in the composition of the build-up of defence forces required in the Middle East to counter any further threats by the regime of Saddam Hussein.

F-111F 70-2406 taxiing in the early morning mist on 23 August 1990 for the flight to Taif AB, Saudi Arabia, in preparation for the liberation of Kuwait. (Bob Archer)

A quartet of 48th TFW F-111Fs on the runway at Lakenheath early on 23 August 1990. The aircraft were carrying live GBU-15 2,000lb bombs, although the fuses were not inserted, thereby ensuring they were safe when overflying mainland Europe. (Bob Archer)

Intelligence gathering and air defence assets were the first to be deployed to the Middle East, followed by strike fighters. However, there was a need for long-range precision strike elements, with the 48th TFW being selected to dispatch aircraft at relatively short notice. Eighteen F-111Fs departed early on the morning of Saturday 25 August 1990, drawn from all four squadrons. One week later, on 2 September, a further 14 followed. Many had live 2,000lb bombs attached to underwing hardpoints. These included the Rockwell International GBU-15 2,000lb data-linked glide bombs, although the base reiterated that the fuses were not installed, as a safety measure for the lengthy non-stop flight to Saudi Arabia. Of the early deployments, eight F-111Fs were adapted to launch this weapon, with 70 of these munitions eventually being delivered against high priority targets throughout *Desert Storm*.

F-111Fs 70-2404 and 72-1444 on the runway at Lakenheath on 2 September 1990, about to depart for the direct flight to Taif AB, Saudi Arabia. The nearest aircraft has 2,000lb GBU-15 modular-guided glide bombs and an AN/AXQ-13 data link pod to guide the weapons. 'Bagdad or Bust' is chalked on the vane beneath the rear fuselage. The furthest jet has GBU-15 inboard and a 2,000lb low-level laser-guided bomb outboard. (Bob Archer)

F-111F 74-0183 departing Lakenheath in full reheat during November 1989. The aircraft was the only 48th TFW F-111F lost during the seven-month period spent in Saudi Arabia, when it crashed on the Askr practice range near Taif AB on 10 October 1990. A 2,000lb GBU-15(V) captive trainer round is carried beneath the port wing. (Bob Archer)

48th TFW commander's F-111F leading those of the 494th and 493rd Squadron commanders and the 366th TFW boss's EF-111A. Overflying Saudi Arabia, near Taif AB, late in 1990. (USAF)

The aircraft were stationed at King Fahd AB, Taif, where the 48th TFW (Provisional) was formed to enable the Wing to function but with personnel deployed from other locations. A further 20 F-111s were flown eastward early on the morning of 29 November 1990, bringing the total number of aircraft in theatre at that time to 52. December saw yet more F-111s departing, with ten leaving on the 11th, followed by another pair on the last day of the year.

The 48th aircrews, along with hundreds of other deployed personnel, spent much of their initial flying time on familiarisation sorties, as the desert climate and largely empty airspace were considerably different than that encountered in Europe and parts of the USA. Furthermore, the need to prepare attack profiles and practise tactics against a huge and well-defended opponent was paramount. Each crew member had to be declared combat ready for the coming campaign.

48th TFW F-111F 70-2385 fitted with 2,000lb GBU-15(V) training rounds during mid-August 1990, in readiness to deploy to Saudi Arabia a few days later for Operation *Desert Shield*. (Bob Archer)

A GBU-24A/B low-level laser-guided bomb with several chalk messages in the time-honoured tradition. Clearly 'Rock the Kasbah' by The Clash had meaning for this weapon, as shortly after the image was taken, it was delivered by F-111F 70-2386 of the 494th TFS against a target in Iraq. (Bob Archer collection)

With the backing of the United Nations Security Council to force the Iraqis, by any means necessary, to withdraw from Kuwait, the coalition began preparing for a massive air offensive ahead of a ground assault. On 17 January 1991, the coalition air attacks commenced, with hundreds of aircraft destroying primary targets with smart munitions fitted with laser-guided seeker heads and aided by infrared night-bombing sights. A novel innovation employed by some F-111F crews from the first night was to strike hardened targets with two types of munitions. To ensure aircraft shelters, and the aircraft inside, were completely destroyed, the GBU-15 was fired through the roof, thereby creating a large hole. A follow-up strike very soon afterwards, using 2,000lb GBU-10 Paveway II or GBU-24 Paveway III with laser guidance, was fired to penetrate the hole in the roof and completely destroy anything inside the shelter.

On 25 January 1991, reports began to emerge of deliberate sabotage by the Iraqis to the oil well heads at the Al Ahmadi terminal in Kuwait. The Iraqis unleashed oil from tankers into the Persian Gulf while at the same time turning on pipeline taps at the Sea Island loading terminal, releasing millions of barrels of oil. The potential for a catastrophic ecological disaster could not be underestimated. A plan was hastily formulated to surgically bomb the manifolds and stem the flow. The mission was flown on 27 January with five F-111Fs planned, composed of two strike aircraft launching GBU-15s, two more to steer the weapons to the target using the AN/AXQ-14 data link pod to precision guide the weapon and one air spare.

Crews for the mission were from the 493rd TFS, with aircraft drawn from the pool – squadron markings for the participants shown in brackets. The first pair were 72-1446 of the 494th TFS delivering the weapon at supersonic speed, while the data link was guided by 70-2414 of the 493rd TFS. The sortie was unsuccessful, as contact with the munition was lost. The second pair took over the mission, with 72-1452 of the 493rd TFS launching the bomb and with 70-2414 guiding for a direct hit on the manifold. Another GBU-15 launched from 72-1452 also struck a second manifold target. The second data link aircraft was 70-2408 of the 494th TFS, while the mission spare was 70-2404 of the 493rd TFS.

A trio of 48th FW F-111Fs, with 70-2404 nearest, during an aerial refuelling sortie over the North Sea, shortly after *Desert Storm*. (Paul Crickmore)

F-111F 70-2404 marked for the commander of the 523rd Fighter Squadron, on the ramp at Cannon AFB. The squadron designation is in the place normally occupied by the aircraft serial, relegating the latter to the rudder. (Photographer unknown)

Of even more importance was a task which is believed to have been partially responsible for the Gulf War ending. Located to the north of Baghdad was the large underground bunker at Al Taji Air Base. It was known to be a command centre, housing many senior military personnel who were controlling the war from within the complex. The bunker was deep underground (possibly 50 feet) and was almost impregnable to conventional munitions. The USAF needed a special weapon capable of deep penetration, with just such a munition being hastily developed by the US Army's Watervliet Arsenal, New York. Using the barrel from an eight-inch Howitzer, and weighing some 4,700lbs, a single bomb was produced. Test F-111F 74-0186 of the 431st Test and Evaluation Squadron, 57th FWW, from McClellan AFB, delivered the inert device on the Tonopah Test Range on 24 February 1991, which penetrated the ground. Technicians initially gave up searching for the weapon at 100 feet (it was eventually discovered a further 50 feet down in the desert). Interestingly, Eglin AFB, Florida, engineers suggested that even if the weapon failed to explode, the kinetic energy of the 4,700lb bomb travelling at 1,400 feet per second would still have a serious impact upon any structure hit!

F-111F 74-0186 of the 431st Test and Evaluation Squadron, 57th FWW, from McClellan AFB about to deliver the test GBU-28 on to the target at the Tonopah Test Range on 24 February 1991. (USAF)

Above left: One of only two GBU-28/B deep penetration weapons that were used to destroy the Al Taji underground complex on 27 February 1991. Note the chalked messaged from the armourers. It is attached to F-111F 70-2387. (USAF)

Above right: The crew who destroyed the underground command and control complex at Al Taji on 27 February 1991. Lt Col Dave White was the pilot (right), with WSO Capt Tom Himes, who launched the second GBU-28/B, probably inflicting sufficient damage to bring the war to an end the following day. (Bob Archer)

Designated as the GBU-28/B, the military was sufficiently impressed that two further weapons were produced. Such was the urgency, that as soon as the two bombs were complete, they were flown by Lockheed C-141 Starlifter from Eglin AFB, to Taif AB. Personnel report that the two munitions were 'still warm' when loaded onto the airlifter. The two weapons were quickly unloaded and attached to the port underwing hard points of a pair of F-111Fs. With laser guidance fitted, the two F-111s departed Taif, and flew north on 27 February 1991. The large underground target had air vents protruding to the surface. Therefore, the weapons systems officer (WSO) had to acquire an air vent with great accuracy. Due to incorrect co-ordinates, the first bomb released from 70-2391 missed the target. With only one weapon remaining, there was huge pressure on the WSO of the second aircraft, serial 70-2387. Checking and double checking, the young captain confirmed to the pilot that he had the target. He then pressed the weapons release, and after what appeared to be an interminable delay, smoke was seen coming out of first one, and then other vents.

Although no further details have been revealed, the Gulf War ended the next day, so it is highly likely that Saddam's capitulation was assisted by the loss of senior personnel at Al Taji. The GBU-28/B was developed and fielded in just three weeks and proved such a success that further models were constructed, but with purpose-built casings rather than surplus artillery barrels.

The 48th accomplished a remarkable combat success rate during *Desert Storm*, accumulating 2,417 sorties and striking 2,448 targets. The single biggest target group was tanks and armour, with 920 destroyed, mainly using 500lb GBU-l2 Paveway II munitions. A host of other targets were attacked, with the Wing proudly displaying the details on a board adjacent to the F-111 on static display at Mildenhall's Air Fete in May 1991.

The cessation of hostilities enabled the majority of assets to return home. The first 18 F-111Fs landed back at Lakenheath on 11 March 1991, led by the wing CO Colonel Tom Lennon. Several of the aircraft taxied to the parking spots with the crews wearing the traditional red and white Keffiyeh headdress. Another 30 F-111s returned later in the week, although a small number of aircraft remained in theatre to ensure that Saddam, who continued to govern a much smaller area of Iraq, did not cause further aggression. Operation *Provide Comfort* was formed in April 1991 to protect Iraqi Kurds fleeing in the north of the country in the wake of the Gulf War. F-111Fs were part of

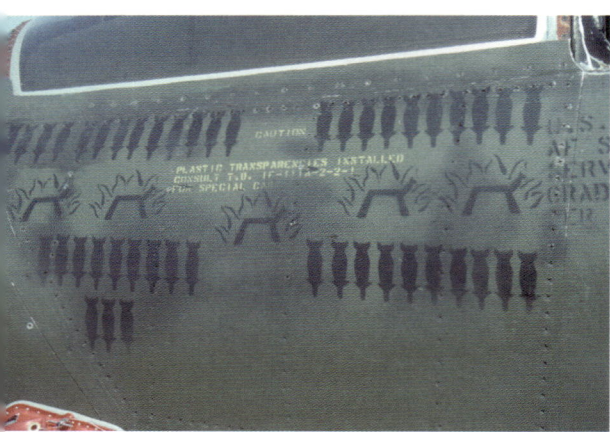

Above left: A WSO wearing an Arabic Keffiyeh headdress as his F-111F 70-2409 taxies at Lakenheath in May 1991, after a prolonged stay in Taif AB. (Bob Archer)

Above right: Mission marks on the nose of F-111F 70-2404 at Lakenheath in May 1991. The kill markings consist of ten laser-guided munitions, eight shelters and a single tank. (Bob Archer)

Left: F-111F 72-1442 with *Desert Storm* combat mission markings, comprising 45 laser-guided bombs and five aircraft shelters. At Lakenheath in July 1991. (Bob Archer)

the 48 aircraft coalition which was operated from Incirlik AB, Turkey to patrol the skies of the Iraqi Northern no-fly zone.

Ironically, no sooner had the Wing returned to something like normality, than preparations began to be made for the F-111F to be replaced with the new McDonnell F-15E Strike Eagle. In readiness for this, the 495th FS, which had conducted operational training, was inactivated on 13 December 1991. Its aircraft were absorbed into the other three squadrons. The Air Force announced that the first Eagles would arrive for ground training purposes, beginning early in 1992, with the two squadrons due to transition to the Strike Eagle by the end of the year. Indeed, F-15E 90-0248, appropriately marked for the wing CO, arrived on 21 February 1992.

During the first few months of 1992, the 48th continued to support the Iraqi air exclusion zones from Incirlik AB and Dhahran AB, Saudi Arabia while at the same time relocating F-111Fs to Cannon AFB, New Mexico, to join the 27th FW. Small batches of aircraft departed at regular intervals. By September 1992, there were just 32 F-111Fs remaining at Lakenheath, although F-15E deliveries were much slower than F-111 departures.

The final four F-111Fs were 71-0888 and 71-0890, both unmarked, while 71-0889 and 74-0178 were inscribed for the 493rd FS CO and 48th FW commander, respectively. These were due to leave Lakenheath on 15 December, but 74-0178 suffered a technical malfunction, with just the first three departing. Following repairs, 74-0178 took off on 18 December, thereby ending the F-111 chapter in the history of the Wing.

The F-111F

Above left: F-111F 74-0178 performed the most combat missions during Operation *Desert Storm*, with 56 sorties flown during 42 days/nights. Forty-six laser bomb symbols are displayed. The nose markings denote *Provide Comfort* operations from Incirlik AB, Turkey. Photographed in August 1992. (Bob Archer)

Above right: 74-0181 of the 524th FS, 27th FW landing at Lakenheath in June 1993. While assigned to the 48th TFW, it flew the greatest number of missions for the 493rd TFS/AMU. (Bob Archer)

Right: 70-2394 of the 492nd TFS with pair of white wings applied to the tail, at Lakenheath September 1989. (Bob Archer collection)

Below: 493rd FS commander's F-111F 71-0889 landing at Lakenheath in November 1992, one month before being transferred back to the USA. (Bob Archer)

Early morning on 15 December 1992, with 71-0889 being prepared for the final flight from Lakenheath to the USA. 71-0889 departed later in the day for the USA, along with two others. A fourth aircraft became unserviceable and left three days later, closing F-111 operations with the Wing. (Bob Archer)

524th FS commander's F-111F 70-2365 landing at Lakenheath in June 1993. Having spent the majority of its flying career at Lakenheath, the aircraft was transferred to Cannon AFB, but revisited soon afterwards, wearing the gunship grey colour scheme. (Bob Archer)

Starting in 1993, 21 F-111Fs were upgraded with Rockwell's Pacer Strike programme to give them a very similar capability to the AMP F-111Es. The 27th was also assigned the responsibility of manning the Operation *Provide Comfort* detachment with its new equipment. Eleven F-111Fs departed Cannon AFB at the end of September 1992 and flew to Lakenheath for a refuelling stop on their flight to Turkey. Interestingly, the F-111Fs retained the Vietnam-style two/three-tone camouflage throughout their assignment to the 48th. However, as soon as they reached their new home, they were repainted in the new single-tone 'gunship' darker grey scheme.

The 27th continued to operate the F-111F for four more years, with 70-2362, 71-0888, 74-0178 and 74-0187 being the final four (see page 73 for details of the ceremony). The first F-111F was delivered to Mountain Home AFB on 14 October 1971, with the last examples retired after a career of almost 25 years.

No sooner had the 48th FW relinquished its F-111s to the 27th FW than the latter staged to Lakenheath during June 1994 with eight aircraft. F-111F 74-0181 is seen taxiing past the old 495th TFS/FS area. (Bob Archer)

Chapter 6
The F-111G and EF-111A

F-111G

The delivery of the first production Rockwell B-1Bs to SAC enabled the FB-111A to be withdrawn from the nuclear mantle. However, instead of retirement, the Air Force chose to convert some surplus FB-111As to a tactical configuration as the F-111G. Clearly, these FB-111As had sufficient serviceability and airframe life remaining to warrant the expenditure of converting from a strategic nuclear role to that of tactical operations. A total of 34 were officially transferred to Tactical Air Command (TAC) prior to conversion, although the new gaining command did not perform any sorties prior to the changes being completed. The transfer was completed in December 1990, with aircraft flown to McClellan AFB for conversion by the Sacramento ALC. Subsequently, TAC was replaced by Air Combat Command, with 19 F-111Gs joining the new organisation. The remaining 15 were sold to

Above: F-111G 67-0162 of the 428th FS, 27th FW at AMARC in November 1993. It carries the name *City of Portales* on the nose-wheel door in black. (Doug Slowiak)

Right: Close-up of the tail of F-111G 67-0162, showing the additional details applied for the 428th TFTS commander. At MCAS Yuma, Arizona, November 1990. (Bob Archer)

After conversion from FB-111A to F-111G, 68-0274 was assigned to the 431st TES at McClellan AFB in November 1991. Later this aircraft was selected for sale to the Royal Australian Air Force. (Peter Boschert)

68-0247 was one of the first two FB-111As converted to F-111G standard, being modified by the SMALC at McClellan AFB. It was subsequently flown by the 2874th Test Squadron at McClellan where it was photographed during September 1992. (Photographer unknown)

Australia, with representatives of the Air Arm travelling to the USA to select the best examples, which were purchased at an advantageous cost. See F-111 Export later for more details.

Conversion to the new configuration was relatively straightforward, requiring the SAC weapons delivery system to be changed to that of conventional and tactical nuclear warheads. The TAC/ACC communications system replaced the SAC equipment. Other, lesser alterations and enhancements were included. The initial two conversions emerged from the modification depot early in 1989 and evaluation began. The two aircraft are believed to be 68-0247 and 68-0254, which were assigned to the 2874th TS at McClellan AFB and the 6512th TS (redesignated to 445th TS on 2 October 1992) at Edwards AFB respectively. Both aircraft were noted at these facilities during October 1989.

Delivery to the 27th TFW at Cannon AFB commenced in June 1990, with the 428th TFTS formed on 1 April 1990 to operate the F-111G solely for aircrew training. However, the squadron began to receive the F-111E from the 20th FW in December 1992, enabling the F-111G models to be retired, a process which had begun in May 1991, with the last departing Cannon in June 1993. Fifteen of these were acquired by Australia, with each being prepared for export at McClellan AFB.

EF-111A Raven, also Spark Vark

The requirement for electronic jamming during the war in SEA during the 1960s resulted in surplus Douglas B-66 Destroyers being modified for this extremely important task. However, the EB-66, as it was known, was vulnerable to enemy air defences and was largely outclassed. Therefore, the Air Force sought a replacement, although the limited number of aircraft required precluded the development and acquisition of a new design. At the same time, the Navy was introducing the EA-6B into service, which the Air Force briefly considered. Apart from the traditional Air Force vs Navy rivalry, the Prowler was primarily designed for aircraft carrier operations and had a crew complement of four. These factors ruled the EA-6B as unacceptable for the Air Force.

Coincidentally, a number of F-111As were available, with an assessment taking place leading to a design prepared for consideration. Whereas the EA-6B had a pilot and three electronic warfare officers (EWOs), the EF-111A, as the newer aircraft would be known, was crewed by a pilot and a single EWO. Grumman was selected as the prime contractor. A formal contract was issued on 30 January 1975 for two prototypes. The first was 66-0049, which was fitted with the 16 foot-long ventral canoe fairing, mounted in place of the bomb bay, designed to accommodate the electronic transmitters and a distinctive pod positioned on the fin tip to house the receivers. This aircraft had no mission equipment installed, being used for airflow evaluation instead. Its first flight was on 10 March 1977. The second prototype was 66-0013, which was fully mission capable and performed its maiden flight on 17 May 1977. The radically new aircraft were assessed by various test organisations, including the Tactical Air Warfare Center at Eglin AFB. This was not a quick process, resulting in operational deliveries not beginning until November 1981.

Two squadrons of EF-111As were located at Mountain Home, along with another at Upper Heyford. The 388th and 390th ECSs were part of the 366th TFW, while the 42nd ECS was assigned to the 20th TFW. On 1 July 1985, control of the 42nd was transferred to the 66th ECW, with headquarters at Sembach AB, Germany, although the squadron remained at Upper Heyford.

During the first Gulf War, five 42nd ECS EF-111As were absorbed into the 7440th Composite Wing (Provisional) at Incirlik AB with effect from 17 January 1991. In addition, 18 366th TFW Ravens

Above left: EF-111A 66-0056 with nose art of a Raven characterised into human form and the legend 'Jam Master'. An additional 'zap' to denote Gulf War One operations: 'Desert Storm – Rockin' Iraq' is stencilled on the nose. (Photographer unknown)

Above right: Tail markings on 67-0034 showing the special identity applied for the AMU commander – the real 66-0042 was lost on 12 February 1969. Note the lightning flash on the receiver pod. (Bob Archer)

366th TFW commander's EF-111A 66-0014 taxiing at Taif AB, Saudi Arabia, early in 1991, with F-111F 74-0182 in the background. The 48th TFW (Provisional) operated all F-111s deployed to Taif as a single 'umbrella' parent unit. (USAF)

42nd ECS EF-111A 66-0016 participating at the Tactical Air Meet at Solingen AB, Germany during June 1988. Nineteen months later the crew of the Raven were credited with the first aerial kill of *Desert Storm* when they out manoeuvred an Iraqi Mirage F1, which subsequently flew into the ground. (Hubert Barnich)

were deployed to Taif and were embedded into the 48th TFW (Provisional) for the duration of their involvement in *Desert Shield/Desert Storm*. A small number of 42nd Spark Varks were also located at Taif.

The only aircraft of the type lost to enemy action was EF-111A 66-0023, which was hit by ground fire on 14 February 1991 while on a mission over Kuwait and crashed in Saudi Arabia. Sadly, the two crew were killed. However, the loss was partially balanced by 66th ECW EF-111A 66-0016, whose crew was being chased by an Iraqi Mirage F1 while jamming enemy radars on 17 January. The Mirage pilot fired two Matra Magic 2 air-to-air missiles, which missed their target when the EF-111A pilot flew evasive manoeuvres while releasing chaff and flares. The Vark was flown down to very low level. An F-15C joined the dogfight, whereupon the chasing Mirage pilot misjudged the situation and flew into the ground. This was the first Iraqi aircraft loss during combat. Rightly, the kill was attributed to the unarmed EF-111A crew.

The F-111G and EF-111A

Nose art of a large predator and the name *The Prowler* on EF-111A 66-0037 at Offutt AFB in July 1987. (Joe Bruch)

The Ravens flew 460 sorties during 1,713 combat hours, which is believed to be the total tally for 42nd ECS aircraft at Incirlik and Taif and includes those with the 366th TFW at the latter air base. The majority of EF-111As returned to their home stations during March 1991, having been replaced in theatre by fresh aircraft and crews to support the no-fly zone (see later). Detachments were ongoing to Incirlik and Dhahran AB, Saudi Arabia to support both the northern and southern United Nations mandated exclusions above Iraq.

On 9 March 1991, control of the 42nd was officially reassigned to the 20th TFW when the aircraft returned to the UK. On 1 July 1992, the 42nd inactivated, with the aircraft gradually returning to the USA.

EF-111As continued to operate at Mountain Home until June 1993, when the remaining aircraft were consolidated at Cannon AFB. The 430th ECS was activated on 1 July 1992 in readiness to centralise all F-111 operations at Cannon within the 27th FW. However, the assignment was short lived, as the unit

Above left: EF-111A 66-0044 of the 27th FW named *Straight Flush* with five playing cards on the nose. This aircraft had the dubious honour of being the last of 120 USAF F-111 of any variant to be lost in an accident or combat when it crashed at Tucumcari, New Mexico on 17 June 1996. (Photographer unknown)

Above right: Very colourful nose markings on 27th FW EF-111A 66-0013 named *Yankee Air Pirate* at Cannon AFB. (Mike Kaplan)

49

inactivated on 29 June 1993 when the 429th ECS moved to Cannon from Mountain Home, as the sole unit operating the type.

Following the withdrawal from USAFE, the commitment to Iraq continued, with 366th and, later, 27th aircraft deploying to the region from the USA. Most deployments were flown to the Middle East with a stopover at Lakenheath for crew rest and any minor maintenance requirements. These temporary duty missions continued until the EF-111As were withdrawn from service. The final pair of EF-111As departed Cannon for storage at D-M AFB on 19 June 1998. The Spark Vark was the last dedicated electronic warfare aircraft in the USAF inventory and was not replaced due to the introduction of stealth technology to new fighter aircraft. Furthermore, most non-stealthy modern aircraft types have incorporated sufficient electronic wizardry to negate any separate specialised requirement.

An electronic crow caricature and the legend *Let 'Em Eat Crow* on the nose of 67-0034 – the wording that has been displayed on several EF-111As. At Upper Heyford in August 1986. (Bob Archer)

Nose profile of the 42nd ECS EF-111A *Ye Old Crow* 67-0035 at Alconbury in August 1987. (Bob Archer)

Chapter 7

The FB-111A

It would probably be fair to say that Strategic Air Command did not really want a modified version of the F-111 as an interim asset pending the acquisition of the Advanced Manned Strategic Aircraft. However, with no alternative, the strategic bomber version was the only choice. GD had proposed two medium bomber models of the aircraft to satisfy the perceived SAC need. The command chose the more simplified example. Designated as the FB-111A, SAC initially wished for 263 to equip more than a dozen operational squadrons, plus another dedicated to crew training.

SAC wanted the new bomber quickly, particularly as McNamara had announced that the Convair B-58 Hustler was to be retired by June 1971. GD modified the 18th RDT&E F-111A to be the development aircraft for the FB-111A programme, followed soon afterwards by the eighth pre-production

Right: 380th BW FB-111A 68-0286 taxiing at Fairford in July 1989. The inscription *Outlaw* is carried on the nose-wheel door, along with the names of the allocated pilot and dedicated crew chief. Two years later, the aircraft was retired and displayed at Plattsburgh AFB and is now preserved in the city. (Bob Archer)

Below: The second prototype FB-111A 67-0160 at Eglin AFB in 1969, loaded with a 600-gallon fuel tank for jettison tests. (USAF)

airframe. The modified aircraft was accepted by the Air Force on 18 August 1967 and commenced a rigorous test programme. Despite some shortcomings, SAC was sufficiently satisfied to order ten FB-111As in 1967, followed by a further 53 in 1968, and a final twelve in 1969.

SAC elected to station the first unit at Carswell AFB, Texas, which was situated across the main runway from the giant GD factory at Fort Worth. The 340th Bomb Group was activated along with the 4007th Combat Crew Training Squadron (CCTS) on 2 June 1968. The first aircraft to be delivered was 67-7193, which joined the unit on 29 June 1969. Having established the primary purpose of introducing the FB-111A into SAC service, the 340th inactivated on 31 December 1971. Two former SAC B-47 wings were in readiness to begin operational status with the new bomber. The 509th Bomb Wing at Pease AFB, New Hampshire, was re-formed on 1 December 1969 and received its first aircraft on 16 December 1970. This was followed by the 380th Strategic Aerospace Wing (changed to a bomb wing on 1 July 1972) at Plattsburgh AFB, New York, which began FB-111A operations in July 1971. The latter wing assumed the training mission when the 4007th moved to Plattsburgh on 31 December 1971. The 4007th was redesignated as the 530th CCTS on 1 July 1986.

Above: 509th BW flagship FB-111A 69-6509 with a red and blue fin tip stripe, for the two bomb squadrons. Both sides of the nose have artwork and the inscription *Spirit of the Seacoast*. Visiting Grand Forks AFB, North Dakota, in September 1985. (Paul Bigelow)

Left: 69-6509 tail markings for both the 393rd and 715th Bomb Squadrons. (Paul Bigelow)

Above: The last FB-111A built was 69-6514, which was assigned to the 509th BW and is seen taxiing at Pease AFB, New Hampshire. (USAF)

Right: Full colour Wing emblem on the starboard side of the forward fuselage, alongside an outline of New Hampshire and a sailor holding a ship's wheel. Named *Spirit of the Seacoast*. (Paul Bigelow)

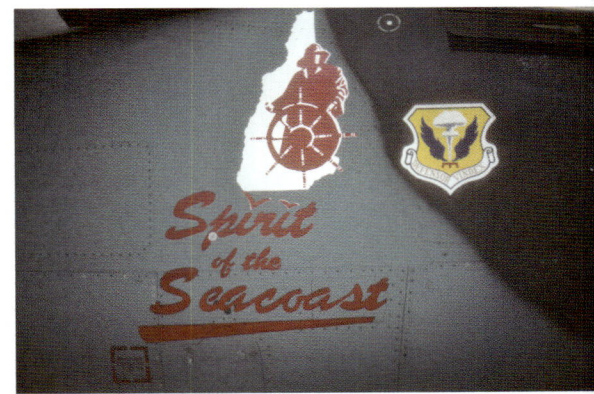

As soon as SAC declared both wings operational, the FB-111A joined the alert force with a small number of aircraft maintained in readiness, situated on the 'Christmas tree' parking area, some armed with nuclear weapons. The FB-111A did not deploy overseas very often, although the type was occasionally included in exercises in Europe and the Far East. Furthermore, the FB-111A did not participate in any combat operations, as deliveries were too late for the war in Vietnam, and it was in the process of being prepared to be withdrawn when the US deployed vast number of personnel and equipment to the Middle East for *Desert Shield/Desert Storm*.

SAC was often quick to remove unwanted assets from the inventory, with the FB-111A being no exception. However, only 17 were retired for storage to D-M AFB, with the remainder being converted to F-111G configuration for a lease of life with Air Combat Command and the Royal Australian Air Force. Those that were sent for storage did so between 6 May and 10 July 1991.

The FB-111As spent much of their lives on alert, parked ready to launch at short notice, while operational flying often involved lengthy training sorties. Therefore, their airframes' lives were lower than those employed for tactical roles. The decision was made to convert 34 FB-111As for tactical operations as the F-111G. The two development aircraft were transferred from SAC for conversion in 1989, with the remainder to TAC between June and December 1990. The combination of retirements and transfers ended the FB-111A's career after 20 years of service.

SAC bombers have occasionally participated in the NATO Tiger Meet. The 393rd Bomb Squadron, 509th BW sent FB-111A 68-0247 to Kleine Brogel AB, Belgium in June 1978 decorated with a black and yellow tiger pattern tail. The SAC Milky Way sash is applied around the nose. (Jurgen Valley)

Left: Tiger Meet participant 509th BW FB-111A 68-0272 at Montijo AB, Portugal in June 1987. The rudder was decorated with a black and yellow tiger pattern, which was in stark contrast to the extremely low-visibility camouflage pattern of the aircraft itself. (Paul Bennett)

Below: Five 509th BW FB-111As, including 68-0273 flew to RAF Waddington during August 1986 for the Tactical Fighter Meet. All five were painted in the new extremely low-visibility camouflage pattern. (Hubert Barnich)

The FB-111A

Surprisingly, the FB-111A was not included in the participants of the RAF Strike Command bombing and navigation competitions held at RAF Marham during the 1970s and 1980s. Two examples, one from each of the two units, did fly to Marham in the spring of 1971 during Double Top 71 to perform some demonstration missions but did not participate in the main event. Subsequent competitions involved only the Boeing B-52 Stratofortress. SAC did not elaborate on the absence of the new asset from the European competition.

However, the version did take part in the Giant Voice competitions within the USA. The FB-111A participated for the first time in November 1970 at McCoy AFB, Florida, with the type performing well. In November 1974, a 380th Bombardment Wing (BW) crew won the Fairchild Trophy while flying from Barksdale AFB, Louisiana. The 1975 event was cancelled due to congressional criticism. In its place, SAC organised Operation High Noon, a short notice exercise for SAC bomber crews flying from their home stations. No FB-111As participated, although the 366th TFW at Mountain Home flew six F-111Fs.

Still displaying the winged 2, to denote the 2nd Air Force, 380th BW FB-111A 68-0279 was a participant at the 1981 Giant Voice competition. (Peter Boschert collection)

366th TFW F-111F 71-0892 with markings applied for the SAC-organised Exercise High Noon during 1975, which replaced the annual bombing and navigation competition due to congressional interference. TAC participated with six F-111Fs. Aircraft photographed at Mountain Home AFB in October 1975. (Bob Archer)

Above left: Large TAC emblem and yellow lightning flash on the tail of F-111F 71-0892 for Exercise High Noon. (Bob Archer)

Above right: Nose markings Spirit of Mountain Home and a silhouette of the state of Idaho on 71-0892. (Bob Archer)

The 380th BW won the Fairchild Trophy again in October 1976, September 1977 and October 1978. Its sister unit, the 509th BW, won the same trophy in November 1979, November 1981, November 1982 and November 1983. In November 1984, it was the turn of the 380th BW again – the only unit to win this award five times. TAC and USAFE F-111s also participated at various times during the 1980s.

Left: Former SAC FB-111A 68-0275 was repainted in a tactical scheme and placed on display at Kelly AFB, Texas, close to the San Antonio ALC. (Paul Bigelow)

Below: 380th BW ceremony for the retirement of the FB-111A at Plattsburgh AFB, New York. Held on 10 July 1991. The Wing was transitioning to just the KC-135 Stratotanker, having been redesignated as an air refuelling wing ten days earlier. (via Terry Panopalis)

FB-111A 67-0159 was assigned to the SMALC at McClellan AFB, California, for much of the 23 years of USAF service. Latterly, an attractive red and white colour scheme was applied prior to joining the Aerospace Museum of California at the base. (Ben Knowles collection)

Unsurprisingly, the FB-111A did not leave much of a legacy, and its passing from service was not mourned by SAC. The final aircraft to be retired to D-M AFB was 68-0249 which arrived for storage on 10 July 1991. The Command itself passed into history on 1 June 1992, with those associated with the FB-111A being reassigned elsewhere with other commands. Therefore, there was little time or enthusiasm to remember the FB with affection.

USAF Ground Trainers

The Air Force utilised a number of development F-111s at technical training schools to teach tradesmen their profession. Apart from no longer having a flying role, these aircraft offered trainees the opportunity to familiarise themselves with airframes featuring modern technology.

Five RDT&E F-111s were flown to Sheppard AFB, Texas, for ground instruction training with the Sheppard Technical Training Center (TTC). 63-9768 was the first to arrive, landing on 4 December 1968, followed by 63-9770 on 1 April 1969, 63-9772 on 21 March 1969, 63-9775 on 12 November 1969 and 63-9773 on 19 November 1969. Initially, these were located on the main ramp at Sheppard, within

Wearing the Air Training Command emblem on the fin, second development F-111A 63-9767 was flown from Fort Worth to Chanute AFB, Illinois, on 4 December 1969. Initially a training airframe, it was eventually displayed at the Octave Chanute Aerospace Museum, where it was seen in October 1993. Following the demise of the museum, the F-111 moved to Waukegan National Airport, Illinois for display. (Bill Peake)

During the 1980s, many ground technical airframes with the Sheppard TTC were repainted in the markings of operational versions in service at the time. Among these was F-111A 63-9768, with the markings of the 27th TFW and the name 'City of Graham' on the nose. Despite being applied by military personnel, as can be seen, the markings are not 100 per cent accurate. However, as the aircraft was a non-flying airframe, it was not considered important. At Sheppard AFB, Texas, in November 1983. (Paul Bigelow)

the huge technical training complex. They retained the pale grey colour scheme carried during their development assignment. However, by 1979, some had been camouflaged with the traditional green and brown pattern. Furthermore, by April 1981, 63-9768, 63-9772, and 63-9775 had large names applied to the port side of the nose: *City of Graham, City of Frederick*, and *City of Vernon*, respectively. By October 1983, 63-9773 had been preserved on base, wearing tail code 'CC', while the same code was applied to 63-9768. By March 1987, this aircraft had the serial presented as 67-27TFW. In October 1988, 63-9768 was still coded 'CC', while 63-9772 and 63-9775 were both coded 'UH'.

During October 1989, 63-9768, 63-9772 and 63-9775 had been joined by the ejection capsule from F-111D 68-0130. The aircraft had crashed shortly after take-off from Cannon AFB on 21 October 1988, with the crew ejecting safely.

By August 1991, 63-9768 and 63-9775 were still being utilised and had been joined by F-111As 67-0046, 67-0047, 67-0051, 67-0056 and 67-0057 all coded 'MO', which had been withdrawn from the 366th TFW. All were retired from operational use with the 389th TFTS and flown to Sheppard AFB soon afterwards. 63-9768 and 63-9772 were moved to a compound near the end of the runway by June 1993, prior to finding new homes. 63-9768 was delivered by road to the military port at Norfolk, Virginia in 1995 and loaded aboard an Australian Navy vessel for transport to Sydney. The airframe was acquired for use as a battle damage repair trainer at Amberley. Later, this airframe was one of the many Australian F-111s which were buried after retirement – see under F-111 Export in the next section. The hulk of 63-9772 was moved to NAWS China Lake, having departed sometime after June 1993. 63-9775 also survived and is preserved at the US Space and Rocket Center at Huntsville, Alabama.

As stated, five former 366th TFW F-111As were relocated here, having been withdrawn from service during August 1990. These were joined by former 20th FW F-111E 68-0027, which departed Upper Heyford on 20 July 1993 for reassignment to the TTC.

Whereas the RDT&E F-111As were operated from the main ramp at Sheppard, the F-111As and the F-111E were moved to a compound nearby, which also contained at least one C-130. During March 1996, the mixed complement of technical training airframes began to apply tail code 'ST', signifying Sheppard Training. All six F-111A/Es were subsequently recoded. However, by the end of the 1990s, the days of the F-111 were drawing to a close, with 67-0057 being placed temporarily on the dump.

Clearly, the F-111 was a popular aircraft, as none of the six was scrapped, with all finding new homes. Five are confirmed as being preserved: 67-0046 at Brownwood Regional Airport, Texas; 67-0047 at Farmingdale RAP, New York; 67-0051 Tyler Pounds RAP, Texas, 67-0057 at Dyess AFB, Texas, and 68-0027 Midland-Odessa Airport, Texas, while 67-0056 was last reported as stored at Sheppard AFB.

F-111A 63-9775 at Sheppard TTC in October 1975. After a short period of development work, the F-111 was retired to Sheppard AFB in November 1969 and remained a ground trainer until relocated to the US Space and Rocket Center at Huntsville, Alabama. While most ground trainers had the unofficial 'G' prefix to indicate non-flying, the F-111s are believed to have lacked this appellation. (Bob Archer)

Former 366th TFW F-111A 67-0051 wearing the tail code 'ST' to signify assignment to the Sheppard TTC at Sheppard AFB, Texas. Parked in one of the more inaccessible areas of the base in April 2001. (Bob Archer)

Chapter 8

The F-111 in Foreign Service

F-111 Export – Royal Australian Air Force

Australia was the only air arm outside of the USA to operate the F-111. At the beginning of the programme, Australia ordered 24 F-111C versions, which were essentially similar to the F-111A model. Despite being completed and each performing their first flight between August 1968 and January 1969, all 24 were stored at the GD Fort Worth facility while technical problems were rectified. In the interim, Australia leased two dozen F-4E Phantoms, which were diverted from USAF stocks from the McDonnell production line at St Louis. The F-4s began delivery on 14 September 1970 and arrived in Australia quite quickly. All were stationed at Amberley, which was to be the home of the F-111s. The Phantoms flew the same mission as the F-111s, with some discussion as to their retention once the F-111s were received.

However, as soon as the F-111 issues were resolved, the aircraft were officially accepted by the Royal Australian Air Force (RAAF) on 1 June 1973 and began being ferried to Amberley between June and December. By the time the first F-111s arrived, some F-4Es had already been returned to the USA, with the final examples leaving later in June 1973. Experience gained with the F-4 enabled crews to transition to the

Four Australian F-111Cs formate with a Singapore Air Force KC-135R off Darwin during a multi-national exercise during August 2004. (RAAF)

ARDC F-111C A8-132 landing at Amberley. The black and white circle ahead of the nationality insignia is to aid focusing when filming weapons tests. (Daniel Tanner)

Right: A trio of Australian F-111Cs headed by A8-146, with a yellow lightning flash on the fin signifying 1 Squadron, while the next aircraft is A8-147 with a blue flash for 6 Squadron. At Amberley in 2005. (Lenn Bayliss)

Below: During 2003 A8-131 had the tail repainted to commemorate 30 years of F-111 operations. (Lenn Bayliss)

Close-up of the tail of A8-131. (Lenn Bayliss)

F-111 more easily, although the latter was more complex than the Phantom. The 82nd Wing operated the F-111s, divided between numbers 1 and 6 Squadrons. Aardvarks flown by 1 Squadron had a yellow lightning flash on the tail, or a large yellow number 1, while those from 6 Squadron featured a blue lightning flash.

Australia experienced flight operations problems with the new aircraft, resulting in four being lost for various reasons between April 1977 and August 1979. One suffered a serious bird strike, while the other three were believed to be engine related, including fires. To redress these losses, Australia bought a further four ex-USAF F-111As, which were delivered between May 1982 and January 1983. They were converted to F-111C standard within country.

Australia Sinks North Korean Vessel

Four F-111s armed with 2,000lb precision-guided bombs sank a North Korean freighter off New South Wales that had been involved in smuggling heroin into Australia. The abandoned vessel was sunk by two of the munitions on 23 March 2006. This was the only occasion when F-111s were used in anger by the RAAF.

Four of the original order were modified as RF-111Cs with a variety of cameras housed in the bomb bay. In addition to the photo reconnaissance role, the four aircraft retained their strike capability. The F-111 successfully continued in service as the primary fighter-bomber, although the Air Force was

A8-126 was one of the original Australian aircraft modified to RF-111A configuration. The camera bay is visible beneath the fuselage below the nationality roundel. (Lenn Bayliss)

concerned that utilisation rates for airframe hours would not extend to the planned 2020 retirement date. To harmonise flight hours, the Australians sought to buy 18 surplus F-111Gs, as these were a similar configuration to the F-111C. A team of RAAF personnel visited the USA in 1992 to choose the best 15 from those available. The Australian aircraft were delivered between September 1993 and May 1994. In addition, the Australians also negotiated for a number of retired F-111s in storage at D-M AFB to be retained as a spares source. These comprised an F-111A, four EF-111As, two F-111Es and three F-111Gs. Beginning in June 2010, the ten aircraft were no longer required and started to be sold for scrap, with HVF West of Tucson, Arizona obtaining the carcasses.

To celebrate 100 years of the founding of Ipswich, nearby Amberly air base painted the tail of F-111C A8-144. (Lenn Bayliss)

Above left: Tail markings on F-111 A8-272, with a skull dressed as a cowboy and the legend *The Boneyard Wrangler*. (Lenn Bayliss)

Above right: Military humour at its best. Crew 5 had this banner made to drape across the nose of F-111G A8-272 when the jet was retired during 2007. (Lenn Bayliss)

A pair of former Australian F-111s being buried in Swanbank landfill site outside Ipswich, Queensland during November 2011. Certain hazardous materials were deemed too expensive to be reclaimed, so burial was the only sensible alternative. (via Queensland Times)

The plan to retain the F-111 in service until 2020 was revised, as serviceability and acquisition of certain spare parts became difficult, despite the source from retired aircraft. Under the new plan, the type would leave the inventory by the end of 2010. The F-111Gs were the first to be withdrawn, being cannibalised for reusable parts, with the last retired on 3 September 2007. The RF/F-111Cs followed, gradually being retired, with a ceremony to officially withdraw the type being held at Amberley on 3 December 2010. The popularity of the type was such that 13 are displayed at various museums or air bases. The remaining 22 were stripped of wings, tail planes, and other components before being buried in Swanbank landfill site outside Ipswich, Queensland, between 21 and 23 November 2011.

The first 24 aircraft featured the Vietnam-style green and brown camouflage, although this changed to a gunship grey towards the latter period of service. The additional 15 F-111Gs were also delivered in the grey colour scheme. Several aircraft were decorated for various milestones in the F-111s career and for specific events.

Above: Australian F-111 commemorating 20 years of operations of the type by 6 Squadron. (David Riddel)

Right: Tail markings on F-111C A8-131 at Nellis AFB, 2002. (Paul Negri)

Above left: The tail of F-111G A8-274 with special markings for 90 years of 6 Squadron. (Lenn Bayliss)

Above right: F-111G A8-274 with artwork for 6 Squadron's 60th anniversary. (Lenn Bayliss)

Left: A8-125 decorated to denote 25 years of F-111 operations during 1998. (Lenn Bayliss)

The RAAF commemorated their 75th anniversary during 1996 with several aircraft appropriately inscribed including F-111G A8-281. (Lenn Bayliss)

The British F-111

The Royal Air Force showed great interest in the F-111 following the ill-conceived cancellation of the British Aircraft Corporation TSR-2 by the Labour Government of Harold Wilson on 6 April 1965. Instead, the Defence Secretary Dennis Healey suggested the RAF acquire 50 F-111Ks, which was a combination of the F-111A and C capabilities. However, the UK government did not have the same degree of faith in the F-111 problems being solved, with the programme being cancelled on 16 January 1968.

The UK Ministry of Defence was in urgent need of a strike capability, as several years of stagnation in the acquisition process had left the RAF with a large gap in this particular role. Coincidentally, the Fleet Air Arm had already selected the Phantom as their new fighter, with more than 140 planned. During 1964, the Navy placed an order for two YF-4K versions, which were designated as the Phantom FG.1 in UK service. This was followed by orders for a further 50 placed in 1965 and 1966. The loss of the TSR-2 and F-111 forced the RAF to accept the F-4 as the most suitable alternative. The first two were designated as the YF-4M, while the remaining 116 were the F-4M. Again, in UK service they were known as the Phantom FGR.2. The Phantom was flown by the RAF in the strike role until the arrival of the SEPECAT Jaguar, when the Phantom switched to air defence as the primary mission. The Phantom served the UK well, being operational until 1992. The F-111 was more complex than the Phantom, although how successful the former would have been in UK service will never be known.

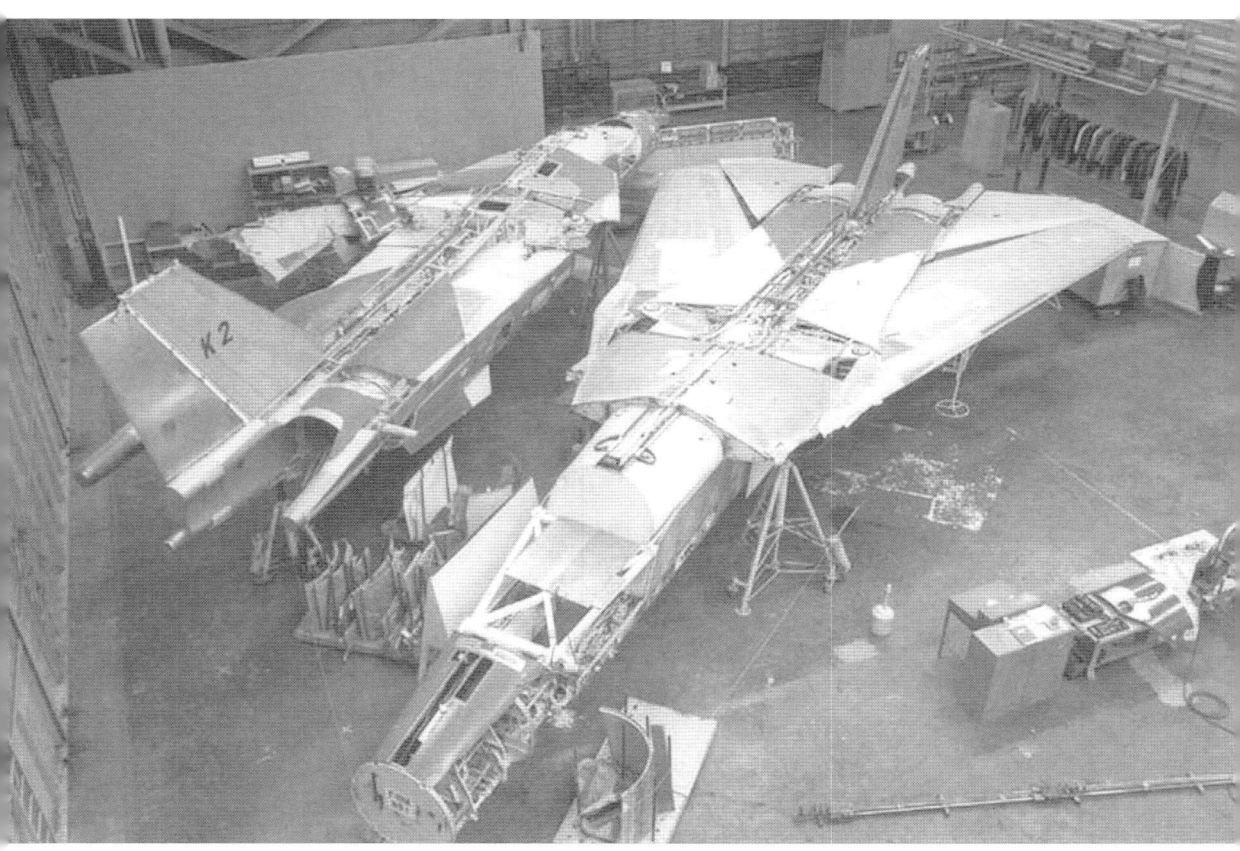

F-111Ks XV884 and XV885 under construction at Fort Worth during November 1967. This was as far as the assembly went, as the cancellation of the RAF order halted any further work. (GD)

What might have been. Imperial War Museum TSR-2 XR222 parked alongside F-111E 67-0120 at Duxford in January 1994. The two jets have a distinct similarity 'at the pointy end'. (IWM)

The first two examples, XV884 and XV885, had completed factory mating of the fuselage sections and were in the process of final assembly. The first completed this process by September 1967, while the second followed by December 1967. However, the cancellation of the programme soon afterwards resulted in the aircraft being dismantled, with major subsystems being transported to the Sacramento Air Material Area for reuse. Other components were used for structural test purposes or to repair damaged aircraft, while the residue was scrapped.

The UK Ministry of Defence allocated serials XV884 to XV887 for the trainer TF-111K version (with USAF identities 67-0151 to 67-0153, and 67-0155) and XV902 to XV947 for the F-111K strike version (with USAF serials 67-0149/0150, 67-0154, 67-0156 to 67-0158, 68-0181 to 68-0210, and 68-0229 to 68-0238).

Chapter 9
Final Days

NASA

The availability of surplus development F-111s, enabled NASA to acquire four examples for various research programmes. All four were stationed at Edwards AFB, with the Dryden Flight Research Center. Three pre-production F-111As and an F-111E were involved in the investigation of various phases of fight characteristics, as well as assisting in solving some of the technological issues which had beset the type earlier. A range of redesigns were incorporated, and flown by test pilots, within the ideal conditions of the desert regions of central California.

F-111As 63-9771, 63-9777 and 63-9778, along with F-111E 67-0115 were the four aircraft involved. The three F-111A models were all flown in the standard grey and white colour scheme which was applied by the manufacturer. At the completion of their test duties, the first pair were retired to D-M AFB for storage in 1969 and 1971 respectively. 63-9771 was subsequently removed from store and air freighted by Lockheed C-5 Galaxy to Cannon AFB on 6 June 1972 for display. 63-9777 was eventually sold for scrap. 63-9778 changed designation to become an NF-111A and was involved in joint USAF/NASA supercritical wing development. Unlike the previous pair, whose flying careers were brief, 63-9778 flew for more than 20 years before being preserved with NASA at Edwards AFB. 67-0115 was the first production F-111E and flew development work with the Air Force before being loaned to NASA. As such, the aircraft retained the three-tone green and brown camouflage. The F-111E was with NASA during 1975–76, for fly by wire engine controls development. It later returned to the Air Force for battlefield surveillance radar tests, before acting as one of the B-1 chase aircraft, alongside several Convair F-106 Delta Darts. It retired to the Aerospace Maintenance and Regeneration Center (AMARC) for storage.

A joint USAF/NASA programme performed by F-111A 63-9778 was the Transonic Aircraft Technology (TACT). Seen overflying the California desert while on a sortie from Edwards AFB. (NASA)

Retirement

USAF F-111s were in operational service for around a quarter of a century. Those close to the type will readily agree that the unfavourable reputation during the period of development and early operations was turned around by the manufacturer (and also by those who flew and maintained the aircraft). Seemingly, the expensive (for the time) F-111, which was at the peak of deterrence one day, was placed into storage in the Arizona desert the next. A total of 39 F-111s escaped the baking heat of D-M AFB and are displayed at Air Force bases or museums in the USA. A further three are preserved outside of the USA, with an F-111E mounted on a plinth at RAF Lakenheath but wearing the markings of an F-111F of the 48th TFW. Another F-111E is with the Imperial War Museum at Duxford and an F-111F is preserved at RAF Cosford.

Left: Journey's end. F-111E 68-0049 wearing the inscription '77th Gamblers Last Deal' on the arrivals ramp at AMARC in November 1991, one month after arriving from the UK. (Doug Slowiak)

Below: Around 130 F-111s and EF-111As await the removal of all mission equipment before being sold for scrap at AMARC. (Photographer unknown)

Final Days

The remaining 330 plus airframes were flown into D-M AFB at regular intervals. At the completion of the one-way flight, the crews were met by personnel from the Military Aircraft Storage and Reclamation Center (MASDC), later renamed AMARC, who officially accepted the aircraft along with all necessary paperwork. The process was fairly straightforward and once complete, the delivery aircrew usually returned to their home station. The aircraft itself was soon towed from the operational ramp at D-M AFB to the preparation area inside MASDC/AMARC. Once there, the fuel was drained and all open areas sealed to prevent weather-related damage. With this process complete, the aircraft was then moved to a specific area of the desert, where it was parked, usually alongside many others of the same type. Whereas some aircraft types subsequently found a second career with another air arm, others joined the civilian market. However, most F-111s were declared surplus after a fairly lengthy period in storage. Regular defence sales ensured that military hardware, including aircraft and helicopters, are disposed of following the removal of all relevant mission equipment. Understandably, carcasses are snapped up by businesses which have opened compounds adjacent to D-M AFB.

In the case of the Air Force F-111s, early test examples were flown to D-M AFB from December 1969 onwards. Following the delivery of production aircraft, the need for development airframes ceased, enabling them to be retired. The RDT&E aircraft, along with the ten pre-production examples were

Right: 63-9781 was retired on 29 September 1972 to MASDC at D-M AFB at the completion of test duties. After a period of storage, the aircraft was cannibalised of all useable parts, before being sold for scrap. (via Steve Hill)

Below: A pair of pre-production F-111s at D-M AFB, after being stripped of all reusable parts. YFB-111A 63-9783 was retired in December 1971, while camouflaged F-111A 65-5708 conducted tests at Eglin AFB, Florida, before being withdrawn on 30 March 1971. (AMARC)

constructed to a different configuration from production versions. Therefore, it would not have been cost effective to upgrade the survivors to operational configuration. A dozen were retired to D-M AFB, with the majority being sold to a private contractor for scrap. The remainder were transferred to other military facilities for non-operational ground duties.

During November 1989, the Berlin Wall was breached. This single symbolic act enabled Soviet dominance within Eastern Europe to evaporate, leading to the majority of satellite nations becoming independent and eventually the Soviet Union itself breaking up. Furthermore, former adversaries now became allies as the Cold War dissolved along with the Warsaw Pact. The removal of the tense stand-off across a divided Europe allowed most NATO nations to significantly reduce their military composition. The USAFE was included in this wholesale reduction. The two wings of F-111s were among the units which no longer had an effective role.

Whereas the 20th FW was transferred home, and Upper Heyford closed, the 48th FW at Lakenheath, with four squadrons of F-111Fs, fared differently. Instead of being inactivated following the retirement of the 80 plus aircraft, the Wing was slated to switch to two versions of the McDonnell Douglas F-15 Eagle. The 493rd FS transitioned to the F-15C/D version, assuming the air defence mission, while

The marking applied to the nose of F-111F 74-0178 prior to scheduled departure from Lakenheath on 15 December 1992 (although the aircraft suffered a fuel leak and actually departed on 18 December). The special design incorporates the flags of the Allied nations which the 48th supported while deployed to the Middle East for various United Nations air exclusion zones. The three flags at the top of the design are Libya, Iraq and Kuwait, to denote the nations which saw major combat by the F-111F. The reference to 1977–1992 is the period when the version was flown by the Wing. (Bob Archer)

Seventy F-111/EF-111As in storage during October 1999. These were the last examples that were retired, and the majority are in the grey colour scheme. (Peter Boschert)

the 492nd and 494th FSs gained the F-15E Strike Eagle, thereby retaining the fighter-bomber role. The fourth squadron, the 495th FS, had performed the aircrew training role and was therefore the first and only unit to inactivate. This commenced in December 1991. The 492nd FS sent their F-111s home beginning in May 1992, with the 494th following from October 1992. The 493rd FS completed the process in December 1992.

Despite no longer having a role within USAFE, the F-111F remained a highly capable weapons delivery platform. Therefore, instead of being retired, more than 70 were transferred to the 27th FW, assigned to three squadrons. The delivery of the newer version, which began in May 1992, enabled the F-111D model to be retired. However, the F-111F had only a short-term career in New Mexico, as the F-16C/D began to arrive with the 27th. The acquisition of newer equipment enabled the F-111 to begin the retirement process in October 1995, with this being completed at the end of July 1996.

The final four aircraft departed Cannon AFB and flew to Fort Worth for a retirement ceremony. The event was staged between 26 and 28 July 1996 as a reunion for former F-111 aircrew, maintainers and other personnel associated with the type. For the occasion, the nose of 524th FS F-111F 74-0187 was decorated with a Statue of Liberty and 'FAREWELL', while streamers for combat operations *Constant Guard V – Combat Lancer, El Dorado Canyon*, and *Desert Storm* were in place. Tail codes of the primary operators were also applied to the large nose decoration, while '380th BW' and '509th BW' represented SAC. 74-0187 was selected as this was the second from last F-111 built – the final example being 74-0188 which was lost in an accident on 26 April 1983. The other three aircraft were 70-2362, 71-0888 and 74-0178. The four departed Fort Worth on 29 July bound for D-M AFB, and storage.

Nose markings applied to F-111F 74-0187 for the retirement of the final four fighter-bomber versions at Fort Worth, Texas during July 1996. Some of the artwork had peeled off during the short flight from Cannon AFB to the ceremony. (Gale Larson)

Despite having the honour of wearing the nose inscription at the retirement ceremony of the strike version, F-111F 74-0187 was not spared the ignominious status of being plastered in protective coating when stored at AMARC. All too quickly, the Arizona heat combined with a lack of a crew chief's tender loving care had taken its toll on the paint scheme. The aircraft is now preserved at the Indie Motorsport Ranch in Willcox, Arizona. (Peter Boschert)

After spending considerable time under the baking heat of the Arizona sun, the paint schemes of various F-111s stored at AMARC have been bleached. Cannibalisation has also taken its toll. (AMARC)

Chapter 10

Conclusion

From First to Last

The first pre-production F-111A flew on 21 December 1964, while the final aircraft in service were a pair of EF-111As, retired on 19 June 1998. During the intervening 34 years, the Aardvark went from problem child to successful adult. But the road to success was initially paved with difficulties, involving many man hours to redesign problem areas and a great deal of money. Nevertheless, the F-111 was undoubtedly an important deterrent in preventing forces of the Soviet Union and its allies from mobilising and crashing through Germany's Fulda Gap, and other strategic crossing points, to try to conquer Western Europe. The prospect of 170 F-111s, armed with conventional or nuclear weapons swooping across the Netherlands and West Germany at treetop level to attack targets in the Deutsche Demokratische Republik (German Democratic Republic) DR, Poland, Czechoslovakia and other Iron Curtain countries, was an important aspect in preventing such a Soviet attack. No doubt other NATO assets were also a serious deterrent factor, although without gaining access to the inner most thinking of the hierarchy within the Kremlin, such deliberation will never be known!

Even today, F-111s displayed in museums and/or preserved at air bases appear extremely modern. The long, pointed nose and swept wings would not look out of place on any flight line. However, the technology, which was so troublesome in the 1960s, has been superseded by stealth coating. The three-tone camouflage of the F-111, along with the colour added to the fuselage and tails to display squadron and wing insignia, is far more welcomed by enthusiasts than the dull, dark grey scheme of the present-day fighters. For enthusiasts and photographers, middle-aged aviation glamour will always be far more welcomed than teenage stealth with acne. However, pilots of the teenager would argue that its capabilities are far more advantageous than the swing-wing gladiator of the second half of the twentieth century.

Prior to being named *Red Lady II*, F-111E 68-0077 was inscribed *June Nite*. At Upper Heyford in August 1986. (Bob Archer)

F-111 Colour Schemes

The majority of the RDT&E F-111As, along with the pre-production aircraft were painted in a light grey colour scheme overall. The full colour star and bar was applied on the fuselage, with the serial number displayed on the tail in black. However, at least one of these F-111As was operated in a natural metal finish.

Tiger F-111E 68-0049 landing at Upper Heyford in July 1991. (Stuart Lewis)

Tiger tail F-111E 68-0049 specially marked for the mini Tiger Meet staged to coincide with the Royal International Air Tattoo at Fairford in July 1991. (Bob Archer)

Tail markings on 68-0049.
(Bob Archer)

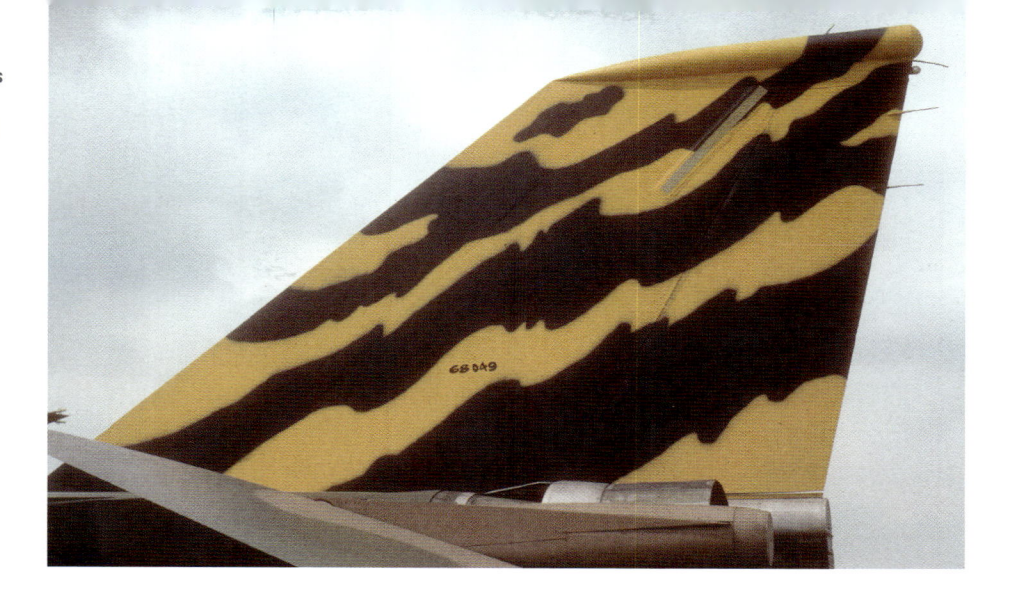

A tiger's head embellishing the nose on 68-0049. The 20 bomb markings were from Operation *Proven Force*, over northern Iraq early in 1991.
(Bob Archer)

Beside the artwork, 68-0049 has the mission symbols applied in white. Most other 20th TFW F-111s had their mission tally applied in brown.
(Ray Sumner)

F-111F 70-2417 with a multicoloured fin tip and the number 1 at Lossiemouth in June 1981 for a joint UK–US tactical bombing competition. (Kevin Wyatt)

Due to their requirement to perform effectively at low level during combat, all tactical F-111s were painted in the three-tone mid-green, dark green and tan SEA camouflage. Initially, the underside was in an off-white colour, although this was replaced by a wraparound camouflage circa 1980. The while tail code and serial were changed to matt black during a similar timeframe. While most tactical fighter/tactical reconnaissance aircraft began to be repainted in the European One dark green and very dark grey (almost black) pattern during the 1980s, the F-111s were spared this extremely unattractive scheme. Whereas stateside F-111A and F-111D models had hard-edged patterns and were virtually identical between aircraft, European-based F-111Es and F-111Fs had soft-edge blending.

At the very end of their careers, the F-111E, F-111F and F-111G models, which were reassigned from USAFE/SAC to ACC, were repainted in a gunship-grey scheme. While it may seem strange to adopt a radical change in colour scheme for just a limited period, the reasoning was simply that the Air Force no longer embraced the Vietnam three-tone camouflage. The gunship colour began to be applied during the late 1980s and was commonplace for stateside aircraft from 1990 onwards. Conversely, the

Gulf War veteran 66-0057 displays 40 mission symbols beneath the cockpit. Adjacent is a small stencil 'Desert Storm – Rockin' Iraq', with camel artwork shown on the engine air intake. Assigned to the 366th TFW and flying from Taif AB, seen over the Mediterranean Sea while returning to the USA at the completion of combat operations. (Jean-Francois Lipka)

F-111F 71-0890 of the 27th FW departing Lakenheath in June 1993. This aircraft left Lakenheath on 20 November 1992, for reassignment to the 27th FW. Repainted in the gunship grey scheme, before returning to Europe a few months later. (Bob Archer)

EF-111A flew for their entire service career wearing a two-tone grey scheme, which was similar to that applied to the EC-130H Compass Call version of the Hercules.

Due to its strategic offensive role, the FB-111A was given a different camouflage pattern, despite the fact that the SAC version was also intended to conduct its mission at low level. SAC wanted its aircraft to appear different from the tactical version, which was readily apparent anyway, as the lengthened fuselage and extended wing tips required to accommodate extra fuel were clearly obvious. The first FB-111A operational scheme was a variation on the green and tan SEA pattern, with a full colour star and bar. The underside was white – a legacy from the B-47/B-52 – as this anti-flash was applied to the two large bombers to help deflect the glare from a nuclear weapons explosion. Subsequently, a very low-visibility dark green/dark grey wraparound pattern was applied, with unit and command emblems presented in outline form. Despite this toned-down scheme, many aircraft were given full colour nose art.

Upon conversion from FB-111A to F-111G standard, the aircraft were amongst the first to be repainted in gunship grey, as Air Combat Command wished to rid the aircraft of all traces of their previous operator's ownership! The majority were repainted at Cannon AFB, with each aircraft taking about one week. All surviving F-111E, F-111F and F-111G models also received this new scheme.

F-111 Final Bow

At the beginning of Operation *Desert Shield*, the USAF had approximately 320 F-111/EF-111As operational – this total not including test or development aircraft. However, by the time the opening sorties of Operation *Desert Storm* began, around one third of the fleet were on station in eastern Turkey and southern Saudi Arabia. During the 43 days of the war, the 90 or so tactical F-111E and F-111F models flew some 2,500 combat sorties. This equates to almost 60 per day, which is a remarkable achievement. The mission capability rate for the 48th was 85 per cent – almost 10 per cent better than that accomplished at home. This was due in no small part to the dry desert climate and the state-of-the-art air-conditioned shelter complexes at Taif.

OPERATION DESERT STORM

amu	sorties	hours	asd	high-flyers
Freedom	651	2522.3	3.87	396
Independence	458	1764.8	3.85	403
Justice	658	2559.3	3.89	181
Liberty	650	2534.8	3.90	178
Totals	2417	9381.2	3.88	48 TFW

Bombs Expended

GBU-10	469	GBU-10I	389	GBU-12	2542
GBU-15	70	GBU-24A/B	924	GBU-24 B	270
GBU-28	2	CBU-87	530	CBU-89	212
MK-12	12	MK-84	146		

Total Expended: 5576   Total Weight: 7.3 million lbs.   Total Cost: $94,835,671.15

Targets

Tanks/armor	920	Towers	9	Buildings	158
Logistics	23	Ships	2	Warehouses	19
SAMs/AAA	25	Artillery	252	Total Bunkers	113
Hangers	13	Vehicles	26	Mine Entrances	4
Runways	13	HAS	245	Pumping Stations	5
Chem	32	Aircraft	4	Personnel/Ammo	67
Bridges	160	IOC's	9	Secondary Explosions	321
Leadership	3	SCUDS	11	Miscellaneous	14

90'   91'

Desert Storm missions scoreboard showing details of the number of sorties flown, munitions expended along with the various types of targets destroyed. The scoreboard was displayed in front of the static F-111F at Mildenhall's Air Fete in May 1991. (Bob Archer)

While being hosted by wing CO Col Tom Lennon at Lakenheath in May 1991, 74-0178 was preparing to depart. With this being the Wing's highest mission aircraft during *Desert Storm*, I asked Tom Lennon if I could photograph it. He simply radioed the tower and advised, 'Hold that aircraft' for me. Such power! (Bob Archer)

By November 1992, 74-0178 had become the wing CO's aircraft. (Bob Archer)

Named *Night Stalker*, and with a fox's head artwork applied to the nose, 20th TFW F-111E 87-0121 is taxiing at Upper Heyford during March 1988. (Andy Thomson)

The four Aircraft Maintenance Units (AMUs) of the 48th, responsible for preparing the aircraft, each had a highest mission aircraft – 492nd AMU nicknamed 'Justice' 74-0181, 493rd AMU 'Independence' 70-2403, 494th AMU 'Liberty' 74-0178 and 495th AMU 'Freedom' 70-2396. The number of sorties completed by these high flyers was in the range of the high 40s and early 50s, with 74-0178 achieving the top score with 56 missions flown. This remarkable aircraft performed faultlessly throughout the campaign and for a limited time afterwards.

Interestingly, the flyaway cost for an F-111E was $9.2 million, while an F-111F was slightly more at $10.3 million per aircraft. This was between four and five times the cost an F-4, although the ability to deliver appreciably more ordnance partially negated the cost disparity.

The F-111 matured from an expensive problem child into a historically significant weapons system whose achievements during *Desert Storm* became the stuff of legends. Personnel who flew, maintained and supported the jets during what became the pinnacle of their capability are proud to have been associated with the F-111. Robert McNamara, who steadfastly believed in the design, was 75 years old when the F-111 went to war in earnest. He was extremely proud to have been party to procuring a product that ultimately became so victorious against such a formidable foe.

'Top Cat' F-111E 68-0030 preparing to launch at Upper Heyford in March 1988. (Andy Thomson)

Appendix

F-111 Tail Codes

Tail codes, or Distinctive Unit Identification codes to give them their official name, adorned USAF tactical aircraft from 1967. Hundreds of two-letter identifiers have been used during the past 50 plus years. First introduced during the Vietnam War, and still widely used today, this fascinating subject has been studied by enthusiasts all over the world.

Despite diligent research by enthusiasts, some of whom are acknowledged later, there remain anomalies that have been brought about for a host of reasons. The F-111 is no exception. The Air Force itself has maintained records but even these are not entirely accurate. Dates of changes of aircraft types, for example, are, in some cases, unclear due to the difference between unit activation and the date when the first aircraft actually joined the squadron. Furthermore, the official records are only as good as the person who compiled them, with paperwork open to different interpretation by the compiler. Nevertheless, the following list is believed to be as accurate as possible.

F-111E with the serial presented as 80045, rather than the fiscal year and the last three. Tail code 'UR' applied, at Upper Heyford in October 1970. (Lindsay Peacock)

Tail Code	Wing	Squadron	Base	Version Dates
AD	3246th TW	3247th TS	Eglin AFB, FL	F-111E Jun 82–Oct 89
CA	27th TFW	481st TFS	Cannon AFB, NM	F-111A Jul 69–Nov 71
				F-111E Nov 69–Jul 71
CC	27th TFW	428th TFTS	Cannon AFB, NM	F-111G Apr 90–Nov 91
		481st TFS		F-111D Nov 72–Aug 73
		481st TFTS		F-111D Jan 76–Jan 80
		522nd TFS		F-111A Sep 69–??? 70
				F-111A Sep 71–Aug 72
				F-111D May 72–Nov 91
				F-111E Sep 69–Mar 71
		523rd TFS	Cannon AFB, NM	F-111D Aug 73–Nov 91
		524th TFS		F-111D Jun 72–Jan 80
		524th TFTS		F-111D Jan 80–Nov 91
		4427th TFRS		F-111D Apr 72–Jan 76
	27th FW	428th FS	Cannon AFB, NM	F-111G Nov 91–Jun 93
				F-111E Dec 92–Oct 95
		429th ECS		EF-111A Jun 93–Jun 98
		430th ECS		EF-111A Jul 92–Jun 93
		522nd FS		F-111D Nov 91–Jun 92
				F-111F Jul 92–Jan 96
		523rd FS		F-111D Nov 91–Dec 92
				F-111F Oct 92–Apr 96
		524th FS		F-111D Nov 91–Apr 92
				F-111G Nov 91–Jul 96
				F-111F May 92–Jul 96
CC	57th FWW	422nd FWS/Det 2	Cannon AFB, NM	F-111A Oct 70–Apr 72
				F-111D ??? 72–Apr 72
		431st TES/Det 1		F-111D Jun 88–Nov 91
	57th FW	431st TES/Det 1	Cannon AFB, NM	F-111D Nov 91–Jun 92
				F-111F Nov 91–Jun 92
				See Note 1
CE	27th TFW	4427th TFRS	Cannon AFB, NM	F-111D Nov 7–Apr 72

Appendix

Tail Code	Wing	Squadron	Base	Version Dates
ED	6510th TW	6512th TS	Edwards AFB, CA	F-111A/D/E Oct 82–Oct 92
	412th TW	445th TS	Edwards AFB, CA	F-111A/D/E/G Oct 92–Apr 93
ET	3246th TW	3247th TS	Eglin AFB, FL	F-111E Oct 89–Nov 92
	46th TW	40th TS	Eglin AFB, FL	F-111E Oct 92–Sep 94
				F-111F Oct 92–Oct 95
HG	347th TFW	428th TFS	Takhli RTAFB, TH	F-111A Jul 73–Jul 74
			Korat RTAFB, TH	F-111A Jul 74–Jun 75
		429th TFS	Takhli RTAFB, TH	F-111A Jul 73–Jul 74
			Korat RTAFB, TH	F-111A Jul 74–Jun 75
JR	20th TFW	79th TFS	Upper Heyford, UK	F-111E Jan 71–Apr 72
JS	20th TFW	55th TFS		F-111E Jan 71–Apr 72
JT	20th TFW	77th TFS		F-111E Jan 71–Apr 72
LN	48th TFW	492nd TFS	Lakenheath, UK	F-111F Jul 77–Nov 91
		493rd TFS		F-111F Jul 77–Nov 91
		494th TFS		F-111F Jun 77–Nov 91
		495th TFS		F-111F Jul 77–Nov 91
LN	48th FW	492nd FS	Lakenheath, UK	F-111F Nov 91–May 92
		493rd FS		F-111F Nov 91–Dec 92
		494th FS		F-111F Nov 91–Oct 92
		495th FS		F-111F Nov 91–Dec 91
MO	57th TTW	422nd FWS/Det 2	Mountain Home AFB, ID	F-111A Jul 77–Mar 80
	57th FWW	422nd FWS/Det 2	Mountain Home AFB, ID	F-111A Mar 80–Dec 81
		422nd FWS/Det 3		F-111F Aug 71–Apr 72
		431st TES/Det 1		F-111F Dec 81–May 88
MO	347th TFW	389th TFS	Mountain Home AFB, ID	F-111F Apr 72–Oct 72
		390th TFS		F-111F Jun 72–Oct 72
		391st TFS		F-111F Jun 71–Oct 72
		4590th TFS		F-111F Apr 72–Jun 72
MO	366th TFW	388th TFTS	Mountain Home AFB, ID	F-111A Jul 77–Mar 81
		388th ECS		EF-111A Nov 81–Mar 84
		389th TFS		F-111F Oct 72–mid-77

Tail Code	Wing	Squadron	Base	Version Dates
				F-111A mid-77–Oct 79
		389th TFTS		F-111A Sep 79–Jul 91
		390th TFS		F-111F Oct 72–mid-77
				F-111A mid-77–Mar 84
		390th ECS		EF-111A Apr 84–Nov 91
		391st TFS		F-111F Oct 72–mid-77
				F-111A mid-77–Jul 90
	366th FW	390th ECS	Mountain Home AFB, ID	EF-111A Nov 91–Jun 92
	366th Wg	390th ECS	Mountain Home AFB, ID	EF-111A Jun 92–Sep 92
		429th ECS		EF-111A Sep 92–Jun 93
MP	347th TFW	389th TFS	Mountain Home AFB, ID	F-111F Oct 71–Apr 72
MQ	347th TFW	4590th TFS	Mountain Home AFB, ID	F-111F Jan 72–Jun 72
NA	474th TFW	428th TFS	Nellis AFB, NV	F-111A Jul 68–Mar 73
			Takhli RTAFB, TH	F-111A Mar 73–Jul 73
			Nellis AFB, NV	F-111A Jun 75–Aug 77
		429th TFS	Nellis AFB, NV	F-111A Apr 72–Sep 72
			Takhli RTAFB, TH	F-111A Sep 72–Jul 73
			Nellis AFB, NV	F-111A Jun 75–Aug 77
		430th TFS	Nellis AFB, NV	F-111A Apr 72–Sep 72
			Takhli RTAFB, TH	F-111A Sep 72–Mar 73
			Nellis AFB, NV	F-111A Mar 73–Aug 77
		442nd TFTS	Nellis AFB, NV	F-111A Apr 72–Jul 77
NB	474th TFW	429th TFS	Nellis AFB, NV	F-111A Jul 68–Apr 72
NC	474th TFW	430th TFS	Nellis AFB, NV	F-111A Sep 68–Apr 72
ND	474th TFW	442nd TFS	Nellis AFB, NV	F-111A Oct 69–Apr 72
		4527th CCTS		F-111A Jul 68–Oct 69
OT	TAWC	4485th TS	Eglin AFB, FL	EF-111A Oct 82–Jun 92
	AWC	4485th TS	Eglin AFB, FL	EF-111A Jun 92–Oct 92
	79th TEG	Det 3	Cannon AFB, NM	EF-111A Apr 93–Sep 96
SM	SMALC	337th TS	McClellan AFB, CA	F-111E/F/G Oct 92–Dec 93
		2874th TS		F-111E/F Jul 92–Oct 92

Appendix

Tail Code	Wing	Squadron	Base	Version Dates
ST	82nd TRW	n/a	Sheppard AFB, TX	F-111A Oct 96–Oct 05
UH	20th TFW	42nd ECS	Upper Heyford, UK	EF-111A Jul 83–Jul 85
				F-111E Mar 84–Jul 85
				EF-111A Mar 91–Oct 91
		55th TFS		F-111E Apr 72–Nov 91
		77th TFS		F-111E Apr 72–Nov 91
		79th TFS		F-111E Apr 72–Jan 91
				F-111E Mar 91–Nov 91
	20th FW	42nd ECS	Upper Heyford, UK	EF-111A Oct 91–Jul 92
		55th FS		F-111E Nov 91–Sep 93
		77th FS		F-111E Nov 91–Sep 93
		79th FS		F-111E Nov 91–Jun 93
UH	66th ECW	42nd ECS	Upper Heyford, UK	EF-111A Jul 85–Jan 91
UR	20th TFW	79th TFS	Upper Heyford, UK	F-111E Sep 70–Jan 71
US	20th TFW	55th TFS	Upper Heyford, UK	See Note 2
UT	20th TFW	77th TFS	Upper Heyford, UK	See Note 2
WA	57th FWW	422nd FWS	Nellis AFB, NV	F-111A Apr 72–Apr 77
				F-111E Apr 72–Apr 77
				F-111E Mar 80–Oct 80
				F-111F Jun 72–Apr 77
				F-111F Mar 80–Oct 80
		422nd FWS/Det 2	McClellan AFB, CA	F-111D Apr 72–Apr 77
				F-111E Apr 72–Apr 77
		422nd FWS/Det 3	McClellan AFB, CA	F-111D/E/F Mar 80–Oct 80
		431st FWS	McClellan AFB, CA	F-111D/E/F Oct 80–Dec 81
		431st TES	McClellan AFB, CA	F-111D/E/F Dec 81–Nov 91
	57th TTW	422nd FWS	Nellis AFB, NV	F-111A Apr 77–Jul 77
				F-111E Apr 77–Mar 80
				F-111F Apr 77–Mar 80
		422nd FWS/Det 2	McClellan AFB, CA	F-111D Apr 77–Aug 77
				F-111E Apr 77–Aug 77
		422nd FWS/Det 3	McClellan AFB, CA	F-111D/E/F Aug 77–Mar 80

Tail Code	Wing	Squadron	Base	Version Dates
	57th FW	431st TES	McClellan AFB, CA	F-111D Nov 91–Jun 92
				F-111F Oct 91–Jun 92
				F-111G ??? ??–Jun 92
WF	4525th FWW	4539th FWS	Nellis AFB, NV	F-111A Jul 68–Oct 69
	57th FWW	422nd FWS	Nellis AFB, NV	F-111A Oct 69–Apr 72
				F-111E ??? 70–Apr 72

Note 1 – The 57th FW F-111s at Cannon AFB were part of the USAF Fighter Weapons School – F-111 Division – and after June 1992 were supported by the 524th TFTS, wearing tail code 'CC' and indistinguishable from those of the 27th FW.

Note 2 – Tail codes 'UR'/'US'/'UT' were allocated to the 20th TFW during 1970, but only 'UR' was actually applied.

Abbreviations Used Within the Tail Code Listing:

AWC	Air Warfare Center		TES	Test & Evaluation Squadron
CCTS	Combat Crew Training Squadron		TFRS	Tactical Fighter Replacement Squadron
Det	Detachment		TFS	Tactical Fighter Squadron
ECS	Electronic Combat Squadron		TFTS	Tactical Fighter Training Squadron
FS	Fighter Squadron		TFW	Tactical Fighter Wing
FW	Fighter Wing		TRW	Training Wing
FWS	Fighter Weapons Squadron		TS	Test Squadron
FWW	Fighter Weapons Wing		TTW	Tactical Training Wing
SMALC	Sacramento Air Logistics Center		TW	Test Wing
TAWC	Tactical Air Warfare Center		Wg	Wing
TEG	Test & Evaluation Group			

Carrying tail code 'JR', F-111E 68-0011 of the 79th TFS, during transit between Upper Heyford and major overhaul at McClellan AFB. (via Steve Hill)

Appendix

F-111E 68-0004 wearing tail code 'JS' of the 55th TFS. At Wright-Patterson AFB, Ohio. (via Steve Hill)

A third of the squadron-allocated tail codes was 'JT' of the 77th TFS on 68-0005. (via Steve Hill)

F-111F 70-2376 of the 366th TFW wearing additional markings for the US bicentennial, at Fairchild AFB, Washington, during mid-1976. The nose inscription reads 'Spirit of 76', while the last two digits of the serials have been incorporated into the bicentennial theme. (Robert Karlowsky)

67-0106 carrying the squadron allocated tail code 'NB' for the 429th TFS. At Nellis AFB April 1970. (Tom Brewer)

Appendix

Flamboyant tail markings of the 430th TFS on F-111A 67-0034 with tail code 'NC'. Again, at Nellis AFB in November 1969. (Roy Lock)

'ND' tail code on F-111A 67-0033 belongs to the 442nd TFS. At Nellis AFB April 1970. (Tom Brewer)

F-111: Fort Worth Swinger

Second prototype EF-111A 66-0013 coded 'OT' served with the 4485th Test Squadron, as part of the Tactical Air Warfare Center at Eglin AFB, Florida. While operational squadrons were beginning to transition to the new Raven, the TAWC was developing capabilities to enhance tactics. (Wally Van Winkle)

F-111E 68-0045 shortly after delivery to the 79th TFS at Upper Heyford on 12 September 1970. Tail code 'UR' was only carried for four months. (Lindsay Peacock)

Another 'WF' coded F-111A, 66-0048, at Nellis AFB in November 1968. (Bill Currie)

SAC FB-111A Units

The first unit was the 340th Bombardment Group (BG) at Carswell AFB, which ushered the FB-111A into service, with an eventual complement of some 30 aircraft. The group inactivated in December 1971, having transferred the majority of its assets to the 380th Strategic Aerospace Wing (SAW) at Plattsburgh AFB. The 380th changed to a bombardment wing in July 1972. In the meantime, the 509th BW had formed as the second wing. The 380th continued operations, flying the KC-135 as an air refuelling wing before inactivating. It re-formed as the 380th Air Expeditionary Wing at Al Dhafra, UAE. The 509th inactivated before re-forming as the sole Northrop B-2A Wing.

Wing	Squadron	Base	Dates
340th BG	9th BS	Carswell AFB, TX	Jul 69–Dec71
	4007th CCTS		Jun 68–Dec 71
	4111th BS		Jul 68–Jul 69
380th SAW	528th BS	Plattsburgh AFB, NY	Jul 71–Jul 72
	529th BS		Jan 71–Jul 72
	4007th CCTS		Dec 71–Jul 72
380th BW	528th BS	Plattsburgh AFB, NY	Jul 72–Jul 91
	529th BS		Jul 72–Sep 91
	530th SBTS		Jul 86–Jan 87

F-111: Fort Worth Swinger

Wing	Squadron	Base	Dates
	530th CCTS		Jan 87–Jul 91
	4007th CCTS		Jul 72–Jul 86
509th BW	393rd BS	Pease AFB, NH	Jan 70–Sep 90
	715th BS		Jan 70–Sep 90

Abbreviations Used Within the SAC Unit Listing:

BG	Bombardment Group	CCTS	Combat Crew Training Squadron
BS	Bombardment Squadron	SAW	Strategic Aerospace Wing
BW	Bombardment Wing	SBTS	Strategic Bombardment Training Squadron

Parked on the vast apron at Plattsburgh AFB, New York, in April 1987, FB-111A 68-0256 is painted in the original camouflage pattern. The aircraft was in service for almost 21 years before being retired in July 1991, having achieved an amazing 6,000 flight hours. (via Steve Hill)

Initial SAC camouflage, with high visibility nationality roundel and unit emblem, 380th BW 69-6513 visiting Bergstrom AFB, Texas, in August 1986. (Peter Wilson)

Appendix

Arguably the most hideous colour scheme ever applied to an Aardvark, 380th BW FB-111A 67-0161 at Hill AFB, Utah. The camouflage is a slate grey and a dark green, although seemingly the two colours blend into one. (Photographer unknown)

F-111Fs 70-2415 and 70-2390 in formation over the North Sea in September 1979. (Paul Crickmore)

An F-111F landing into the sunset on a winter's afternoon at RAF Lakenheath. (Collin Collis)

Further reading from Key Publishing

As Europe's leading aviation publisher, we also produce a wide range of market-leading magazines.

Visit: shop.keypublishing.com for more details

KEY.AERO Your Aviation Destination - Visit www.Key.Aero today